Sex
and the mentally
handicapped

By the same authors

Handicapped Married Couples

Sex
and the mentally
handicapped

A guide for parents
and carers

Michael and Ann Craft

REVISED EDITION

Routledge & Kegan Paul
London, Boston, Melbourne and Henley

First published in 1978
Revised edition first published in 1982
by Routledge & Kegan Paul Ltd
39 Store Street, London WC1E 7DD,
9 Park Street, Boston, Mass. 02108, USA,
296 Beaconsfield Parade, Middle Park,
Melbourne, 3206, Australia, and
Broadway House, Newtown Road,
Henley-on-Thames, Oxon RG9 1EN
Completely reset in 11 on 12 pt Baskerville by
Academic Typing Service, Gerrards Cross, Bucks
and printed in Great Britain by
The Thetford Press Ltd, Thetford, Norfolk

Library of Congress Cataloging in Publication Data

Craft, Michael John

Sex and the mentally handicapped.
Includes bibliographical references.
1. Mentally handicapped--Sexual behavior.
I. Craft, Ann.   II. Title   [DNLM:
1. Education of mentally retarded. 2. Mental
retardation--Rehabilitation.   3. Sex
behavior.   4. Sex education. HQ 54 C885s]
HQ30.5.C7   1982   306.7'0880826   82-5297

ISBN 0-7100-9293-8   AACR2

Contents

v

Acknowledgments

We should like to thank all those who have prompted us to write this book, and who have helped in its preparation, in particular: the National Fund for Research into Crippling Diseases, whose research grant enabled us to continue our study of mentally handicapped married couples and explore the field of health and sex education; parents, care staff, teachers, and trainers, who in their concern for the quality of life of those in their care raised and debated many of the issues we have tried to deal with here; the Health Education Council and the International Planned Parenthood Federation for valuable help and encouragement; the many publishers and film distributors whose practical assistance has enabled us to review audiovisual resources; Mrs Alice Clark, whose secretarial assistance has been much appreciated; and lastly, the mentally handicapped themselves, whose capacity for living and loving is so often greater than we allow.

Introduction to the revised edition

In writing the original edition of this book, we had two purposes: firstly, to explain why sex education and counselling for the mentally handicapped were needed and to offer suggestions on programmes and available audio-visual resources; secondly, to illustrate the possibilities and advantages of marriage for mentally handicapped couples. Four years, and many conferences, discussions and consultations later, both purposes are still relevant.

Many parents and professionals are still fearful concerning marriage and particularly the children of mentally retarded couples. Freely available and effective contraceptive methods now make these two areas capable of being treated separately. While our research shows that relatively few mentally handicapped people get married and fewer have children, all mentally handicapped individuals have a biological clock in them that causes physical sexual development together with sexual needs and feelings.

Human sexuality is composed of many strands, one of which is of course physical pleasure and satisfaction. But an equally important aspect is the making and maintaining of close personal relationships. When the opportunities for intimate friendships are denied, so too is the possibility of that enrichment of life which comes from loving, caring, sharing and cherishing another person. Of course, there are risks involved (both to the mentally handicapped and those who care for them), but with education and counselling (of both retarded and carers) these risks can be kept within reasonable bounds. We believe the potential advantages far outweigh the disadvantages.

It is important to make clear at the outset what we mean by the term 'mentally handicapped'. In the past this label grouped together the socially, physically and intellectually handicapped. Even today it can embrace the profoundly impaired who have both physical and mental disabilities, as well as mildly retarded persons who merge with the dull normal in any society. In this book we are specifically referring to those whose abilities lead them to operate at less than three-quarters of average intelligence (i.e. approximately IQ 70), but who are sufficiently verbal and mobile to form close friendships. This includes many genetically impaired individuals, including those with Down's syndrome, who are now known to be capable of far more mental development than was previously thought possible.

Perhaps a third reason for this book can be cited: we believe it has a part to play in encouraging a more normal response to sexuality, that most normal of human attributes, which is shared by handicapped and able-bodied alike.

1

Myths and morals

the literature

The myths concerning sex and the mentally handicapped are many and various, and sometimes conflicting. The range is great: some see the mentally handicapped as sexual innocents, some as sexually depraved. What are these myths and how do they fare in the light of literature and research?

The myth of national degeneracy and propagation of the unfit

Fears that the national heritage of intelligence and ability in England was being eroded due to the overbreeding of the lower, and by inference, duller, social classes, arose just after the Boer War. One-third of the army recruits had had to be rejected, mainly due to the effects of what we now know as 'the cycle of deprivation'. The ruling classes feared that the dull would soon swamp the more intelligent and from this was born a social policy which first advocated isolated and self-supporting colonies for the mentally defective, and later, sterilization to make quite sure this group did not get larger. It must be remembered that the term 'mentally defective' was very widely interpreted – for instance, any young woman receiving a State allowance (Poor Law relief)

1

who gave birth to an illegitimate child could be, and frequently was, certified as mentally defective, and, for the good of the race and the good of her soul, placed in a colony.

'Reproduction of the unfit' was once believed to be the main cause of mental handicap. We now know from large-scale studies of mentally handicapped children that the majority of them have parents who are within the average ranges of intelligence in the population. This applies particularly to the severely subnormal, one-third of whom are brain damaged, another third of whom have Down's syndrome, while most of the remainder are pathological variants due to genetic misendowment, the causes of which are widespread throughout the general population.

The myth of fertility

Are the mentally handicapped as a group more fertile than the general population? Fertility has two aspects: (a) the biological capacity to reproduce, and (b) effective reproduction, or the numbers of children actually produced. With regard to the first aspect, most of the mentally handicapped are fertile at a biological level. There are obvious exceptions such as Klinefelter's and Turner's syndromes. With regard to effective reproduction by the mentally handicapped we have to bear in mind that their social status often militates against their reproducing children. Kirman states: 'in the main the effective reproductive capacity of the feebleminded below IQ 70 is very limited and below IQ 50 it is statistically negligible.'[1] This could well change in the future as more remain in the community, or marry while in care.

To compare effective reproduction we have to look at longitudinal studies. In 1962 the Minnesota Institute of Human Genetics selected 289 defectives with IQs of less than 70 and institutionalized between 1911 and 1918. Then, taking the grandparents of these defectives, they traced all their descendants forward to 1961, in order to compare the defectives with their cousins, etc. In fact, the resulting data cover up to seven generations and include more than 80,000 people. Thus the researchers were able to compare

2

hospitalized defectives with their grandparents' descendants in the community, thus drawing a wealth of genetic and social inferences. When the childless members of the parental generation were included, the mentally retarded – i.e. those with IQs of less than 70 – had the lowest average number of children (2.09) while the group with the highest IQs – 131 and more – had the highest (2.98). Again, opportunity plays a part here.

The myth of degeneracy: handicap among offspring of the mentally handicapped

Are the children of the mentally handicapped themselves low in intelligence? Estimates of the percentage of handicapped offspring from mentally handicapped parents differ tremendously in the various studies[2] (from 2.5 per cent to 93.2 per cent!). The wide variation is due to the different criteria of each study: for example, one rather than both parents mentally handicapped; the type of retardation of one or both parents, i.e. whether there is a hereditary factor present; the IQ level of parents; pre-natal factors relating to socio-economic status (e.g. malnutrition of foetus).

One of the best studies available is that carried out by Reed and Reed at the Minnesota Institute of Human Genetics.[3] The records of the 7,778 children descended from the grandparents described, showed that where both parents had IQs of less than 70 then 40 per cent of the children born to them were retarded, but the *mean* IQ of these children was 74; when one parent only had an IQ of less than 70, then 15 per cent were retarded and 54 per cent had IQs of more than 90; of the 7,035 children with neither parent retarded 1 per cent had IQs of less than 70.

It is now generally accepted that, compared with their parents, children's measured intelligence tends to show a reversion towards the norm[4]; this is as true for the children of very bright parents as it is for those of very dull parents.

Child-care considerations

Can mentally retarded parents care adequately for their

3

children? This is a difficult area to investigate. As Hall points out, 'the skills that constitute adequacy of any parent have yet to be agreed upon'.[5] Mickelson followed up ninety families in which one or both parents had been diagnosed as 'feeble-minded' and one or both had been institutionalized for a period of time.[6] The care given to the children of each family was evaluated as 'satisfactory' (42 per cent of the families); 'unsatisfactory' (32 per cent); 'inconsistent or inadequate' (26 per cent). The relationship between IQ and adequacy of care was not direct: 30 per cent were rated as 'satisfactory' with one parent in the 30–49 IQ range, nearly one-half (46 per cent) were satisfactory in the 50–9 range. Other factors have to be taken into account, such as the number of children, the number of pregnancies, the psychiatric health of parents, the degree of marital harmony, and adequacy of family income (none of the families judged to be giving unsatisfactory care to their offspring had an adequate income).

The large number of factors which need to be examined in any study of the quality of child care given by mentally handicapped parents makes assessment extremely difficult. A history of institutionalization is likely to have some bearing, whether prison or hospital, as inmates tend to lose social skills. Relevant, too, is the availability of support services. To complicate matters further, many of those once labelled as 'mentally handicapped' in childhood gain in IQ as they improve from their deprivation, and may even 're-cover' sufficiently to merge indistinguishably with the general population.[7]

Sexual responsibility

Are the mentally handicapped so sexually irresponsible they need to be protected from themselves and for the sake of society? This was the reasoning which gave rise to the isolated mental-defective colonies. Most unfortunately the very behaviour that was originally feared was shaped by the enforced segregation from the normal emotional patterns of life and from members of the opposite sex. Open masturbation and homosexual activity came to be accepted as regrettable but usual sexual behaviour among the mentally handicapped. Here, society and care staff have been (and still are) guilty of 'double think'. Many – probably most – handicapped adolescents and adults have had no form of sexual education, no opportunity to learn what is 'normal' behaviour in this context. We have progressed since the days when female patients out walking were separated from the males by fifty yards and a member of staff, but there is still a long way to go. All too often in the area of personal relationships the hospital or hostel resident is expected to 'muddle through', and is punished for stepping over boundaries no one has ever clearly spelt out to him. Negative teaching is never very effective unless accompanied by positive re-direction.

There is evidence that the mentally handicapped are no more at the mercy of their sexual impulses than the rest of us. A research project in the USA at a 2,000 bed state hospital showed residents with an IQ range of 40–70 to be capable of remarkable, almost puritanical, sexual self-control.[8] The hospital campus was large and, because of shortages, the staff supervision was not as adequate as the authorities would have wished. There were many secluded areas where the residents could have engaged in any sexual behaviour they wished with little fear of discovery. In fact, although enthusiastic kissing and necking were acceptable according to the patients' own code of conduct, intercourse was usually considered wrong. When it did occur it was condemned by other residents, and felt to be improper by the couple themselves. As the authors remark, the disadvantage of the dating system was 'its awesome power to deflect patients from their vocational training'. What could be more normal!

Sexual offences

It is sometimes claimed that the incidence of sexual offenders is higher among the mentally handicapped than the general population. This is by no means proven. We do know, however, that certain sexual offences are more common among the mentally handicapped – indecent exposure, indecent assault (often involving experimentation with those of similar mental age), and homosexual offences. Unfortunately their partners are often physically below the age of consent even if their mental ages are similar. The normal child soon learns to keep his oncoming sexuality out of adult view, and experiments are usually with his own peer group, who can be expected to keep quiet. Not so the mentally handicapped child, usually quite unprepared for the changes taking place in his body. He frequently fails to keep his masturbatory activities out of public gaze. Worse, the handicapped adolescent boy may well continue to play with his own peer group, that is, boys of his own mental age. In his sexual experimentations he may thus inadvertently break the legal code. Mentally handicapped girls are often not aware of the consequences of their sexuality, and are commonly flattered by advances from older men and confused by modern advertising.

With sex-education programmes, and where legitimate and socially approved channels for sexual expression are available, a decrease in socially unacceptable behaviour might be expected.

Conclusion

On examination, and in the light of evidence, the bases for the myths and fears are not nearly as strong as is popular belief. It becomes more clear that what the mentally handicapped lack is not self-control but learning experience. We cannot really be surprised that behaviour and responses are shaped by environment and experience (or lack of it). For the mentally handicapped over-protected at home or cared for in institutions which are either monosexual or which traditionally segregate the sexes, there is a significant gap in their social learning and development. Where conditions preclude socially approved sexual behaviour, 'deviant' responses become the norm.

Society has altered considerably since the days of the colonies for the mentally deficient. Myths take longer to change.

2

Is ignorance bliss?

Sex education, counselling and family-planning services

Today more and more mentally handicapped people are living in the community, where they are exposed to the same pressures and stimuli as their 'normal' neighbours. For parents, teachers and care staff to assume that the less a mentally handicapped child or adolescent knows about sex the better is a sure way of asking for trouble. The physical and emotional changes which occur in puberty are confusing enough as it is, without compounding them by leaving the adolescent (mentally handicapped or otherwise) in ignorance, punctuated only by negative guidance – 'Don't play with yourself', 'Don't misbehave with a boy or you'll end up pregnant'.[1] Sexual feelings are part of being human – we ignore them at our peril. Those who are mentally handicapped experience many of the same feelings and drives as the rest of the population, but commonly have been left in ignorance as to how to cope with them in a socially acceptable manner.

In fact ignorance is hardly ever bliss. It is often dangerous. Because a whole area of social education is neglected the mentally handicapped are all too likely to lack the skills which would give them some defence against exploitation and enable them to satisfy their social and sexual needs without bringing them into conflict with the law.

It is socially acceptable in our society for a child to show affection by touching and kissing adults, some of whom are strangers to him although friends or relations of his parents. In normal children this behaviour is less and less expected as the child grows up, but mentally handicapped children are often permitted to continue long after their normal siblings. Any visitor to a hospital for the mentally handicapped will have experienced demonstrations of inappropriate affection from residents. Behaviour that is cute and touching from a 5 year old mongol girl, may cause a situation fraught with dangers in a 15 year old one. Indiscriminate affectionate behaviour can so easily be exploited. As we have seen in relation to sexual offences, boys who explore their sexual feelings with those of their own mental rather than actual age, can easily find themselves on the wrong side of the law.

Most mentally handicapped youngsters are perfectly capable of learning that there is a time and place for sexual behaviour. If those who care for them do not teach appropriate behaviour patterns it is unreasonable to expect socially acceptable behaviour. At least one hospital for the mentally handicapped in the 1960s was found to have a high failure-rate among hostel placements because behaviour to which a blind eye was turned in the hospital grounds caused much public outcry when indulged in outside the hostel. Ignorance here meant a return to hospital care with the label of 'sexual irresponsibility'.

A facility with four-letter words is fairly common among mentally handicapped adolescents, and it is easy to assume because of this that they are aware of 'the facts of life'. All too often, while they may know separate facts, they do not link them up to make a complete picture. Parents, teachers and care staff who begin to ask are usually surprised at the lack of knowledge that comes to light.

'Babies? Oh yes, you have to go to hospital to get one.'
'There's only one difference between a girl and a boy – a girl has different hair.'
'He's kissed me ever such a lot. Will I have a baby now?'

8

⌐ Ignorance, then, will never 'solve' the 'problem' of sexuality. It may well compound it. And there is another point which we should not lose sight of, expressed by Johnson: 'Life is likely to be difficult enough for handicapped people without unnecessarily depriving them of the gratifications of close human relationships, including those involving sex if interest and opportunity exist.'[2] What, then, do we teach the mentally handicapped in our care?

Sex education

We are not claiming that sex education will radically alter behaviour. So far not enough research has been done to determine the long-term effects of sex-education programmes on normal or mentally handicapped children. Such programmes are relatively new, both in the USA and in this country, and we are not yet in a position to answer the vital question of whether an increase in factual knowledge carries over to improved behaviour. The few studies that have been done relied on subjects' ability to recall having had sex education. It is extremely difficult to tease out at a later stage the amount and quality of the instruction, and the manner in which it was given (e.g. in a matter-of-fact manner; with some embarrassment; or perhaps a series of negative warnings). While Michael Schofield[3] found that among his sample sex education seemed to have had remarkably little effect on the subsequent sexual behaviour of teenagers, there was evidence that what the schools term 'sex education' may not be recognised as such by the students, for there is often a lack of frankness in the teaching. One teenager commented: 'She used to draw the diagram but she never mentioned the word "sex" or "babies". It was always little rabbits.' There was evidence, too, that formal sex education came too late – many youngsters did not attend to the teacher because they felt (usually erroneously) they knew it all already.

The basic philosophy behind all education is that the individual who is taught, learns, and in learning, internalizes what is taught, with the result that behaviour is directed in socially accepted ways, and his life is enriched. Alan Harris, in his interesting article, 'What does "sex education" mean?'

9

states that sex education, if it is to be judged by the same criteria as other areas of education, has to aim at the maximum possible degree of knowledge and understanding concerning sexual behaviour.[4] He goes on to list what he sees as the necessary tasks of sex education. In summarizing his points we have added comments as they apply to mentally handicapped children and adolescents.

1. To foster the attitude that in sexual relationships, as in all other relationships, the feelings and needs of other people are equally as important as our own.
2. To foster insight into the sexual feelings and needs of other people and ourselves. Without such insight we cannot know how to avoid hurting people, making them jealous, resentful, etc.
3. To teach the physical and biological facts, for when a person lacks information he or she cannot make a free choice. A girl is not 'free' to avoid having a baby if she has intercourse and does not know about contraception. (Where the girl is mentally handicapped she may not even be aware that intercourse is connected in any way with pregnancy. Margaret Mead, the anthropologist, reports a Pacific tribe of average intelligence who had never made this association!)
4. To teach people to communicate about their sexual needs and feelings to their partner.
5. To teach people to get to the stage of forming their own moral principles and having confidence in their own judgements. (This may sound beyond the ability of many mentally handicapped, but often an over-concern for their welfare smothers any attempt they make to become more independent. They learn all too well that other people always know best, and so they are more likely to do anything that is suggested to them. It *is* possible, for example, to teach a mentally handicapped girl that she needn't say 'yes' to something she doesn't want to happen.)
6. To foster people's ability to be alert and sensitive to situations where they ought to stop and think. (Mentally handicapped adolescents can get much out of role-

playing games, which besides making them more aware of the feelings of others can in a sense 'rehearse' behaviour responses to situations they will meet.)

Sex and health education now have a place in most school curricula, although as far as we know no education authorities have so far evolved programmes specifically for their Special Schools. Mentally handicapped pupils stand in as much, if not more, need of these programmes as their normal counterparts do and this gap is currently receiving attention in educational circles. Kempton draws attention to some of the characteristics of the mentally handicapped which make sex education of *special* importance to them.[5] To summarize Kempton:

1. They frequently over-respond to attention and give affection indiscriminately in return.
2. Their judgment may be poor and their reasoning ability limited.
3. The mentally handicapped often do what is asked of them without question, and stand in danger of being used and exploited sexually.
4. Many do not have access to accurate information; their peers are usually equally ignorant.
5. They are likely to be confused and frightened by myths and half-truths because they find it difficult to distinguish between reality and unreality.

Any such programme must set the biological function of sex in its social context. There are morals as well as mechanics involved.

Obviously, like normal people, some mentally handicapped persons are better informed than others. Any programme has to be flexible in approach so that it can easily be adapted to start with what an individual knows and then move on to areas of ignorance. Appendix 1 details much of the teaching material available in this country.

One of the foremost Americans involved in sex education for the mentally handicapped is Dr Sol Gordon. The following is a summary of the points that he suggests need to be put across to care staff, administrators, teachers and the mentally handicapped, in any teaching programme:[6]

1. Masturbation is a normal expression of sex, no matter how frequently it is done and at what age.
2. All sexual behaviour involving the genitals should be done in private. Institutions and hostels not built for privacy should liberally define what is a 'private' area, e.g. one's own bed or the bathroom, as opposed to the 'public' day room.
3. Any time a physically mature boy and girl have sexual intercourse they risk pregnancy.
4. Both should use birth control methods unless both partners are clear about wanting to have a baby and the responsibilities that go with childbearing.
5. It is unlawful to have sexual intercourse with a girl under 16. In general, society prefers people to be adults (over 18) before they have intercourse.
6. Adults are not permitted to use children sexually.
7. The only way to discourage homosexual activity is to risk heterosexual activity.
8. In the final analysis sexual behaviour between consenting adults (whatever their mental age), whether it is homo- or hetero-, should be no one else's business – provided there is little risk of unwanted pregnancy, and both enjoy the experience.

Counselling

Counselling here means responding to specific situations which arise. It should never be merely the giving of advice, for it needs to include an exploration of the situation as the handicapped person sees it, and a working through of the solutions available.

Anyone can find themselves cast in the role of a counsellor – in instances where the mentally handicapped person is living away from his home it is likely to be a care-staff member, or a teacher at the residential school or college. What is particularly important is that the counsellor approached understands the implications of what he is doing. He needs to use words that are understood and to check at each stage that he is making sense.

Care staff and teachers stand in a similar position to parents where the mentally handicapped are concerned. They will almost certainly share the same fears and be as reluctant as many parents to risk letting their charges/ children get into situations which may result in hurt or unhappiness. As with parents, anxiety is often based on *anticipation* of problems rather than actually experiencing them. Risks, however, are part of life and all too often we over-protect those in our care to the extent that we stunt the development of maturity. One of the purposes of this book is to share our belief that some of the risks are warranted because the potential prizes of happiness, partnership and joint enrichment of life are so worth while, and the dangers of apathy, loneliness and atrophy are too common within institutions and without.

The mentally handicapped require careful counselling in the sense that it is all too easy to talk over their heads or bring in aspects which we may see as having a bearing on the matter under discussion but which only confuse them. They usually learn better by concrete experiences or by talking about their own experiences.

One of the hospital married couples in our survey illustrates some of the difficulties of our present counselling programme.[7] During their engagement Gareth and Helen explored with a counsellor the subject of marriage, and the responsibilities it would entail, in depth and in detail. Once they were married, staff assumed all was well until in fact the partnership reached crisis point. The *words*, even the *pictures* used beforehand, did not link up with their *experience*. Gareth was sexually unskilled and his first attempts at intercourse were clumsy. Not surprisingly Helen 'froze', making intercourse impossible. This situation continued for almost a year until they were counselled about their specific difficulties. It was found that Helen was rather small. A minor operation made it physically more comfortable for her. Gareth was prompted to be more gentle, Helen relaxed more, and both gained enormously in satisfaction.

Family-planning services

No special family-planning service exists for mentally handicapped people, and there would obviously be disadvantages in setting up a separate facility. In the USA recently a special clinic was opened on an experimental basis to explore the possibility of providing family-planning services for the mentally handicapped.[8] The study monitored various treatment approaches, staff-training needs, delivery of care, and use of contraceptives. In spite of wide publicity through the mass media and contact with institutions and professionals, the number of clients coming forward was low (47 in a seven-month period, 41 of them coming from one large institution).

In the light of their experiences David, Smith and Friedman make several recommendations for the successful implementation of such a service for mentally handicapped people, and these would seem to be relevant in the British context. They suggest that the service be set up within the normal provisions existing, but that there should be staff in selected clinics specifically trained to work with mentally handicapped clients. They further recommend that training in sex education and family planning be offered to staff in institutions and parent groups, to prepare clients for more effective use of proposed services. Parents particularly need counselling to alleviate their anxieties and to help them consider the possibilities of family-planning services in training their children for life experiences (we shall be looking at this in more detail in chapter 4). As the American study showed, mentally handicapped people are difficult to reach and it would be advantageous to make others in the local community (citizens and professionals) aware of the legitimate needs of this handicapped group, the availability of services, and the benefits that would be obtained from responsible sexuality and prevention of unwanted pregnancies.

In this country the Family Planning Association has been a joint organizer with the National Society for Mentally Handicapped Children and MIND, the National Association for Mental Health, of workshops for professionals concerned with the care of the mentally handicapped. This is a welcome trend.

Sex education and counselling should form an integral part of the training and support we give to the mentally handicapped, helping them to an understanding of their feelings and their bodies. They should also be made aware of the existence and purpose of the family-planning service, with particular information about the site and hours of access of the local clinic. The advantages of dispelling ignorance are potentially great: the enrichment of all areas of life.

3 Psycho-sexual development

'Psycho-sexual' is the term used to convey sexual development in its widest meaning, for our sense of identity, our personhood, is inextricably bound up with our sexuality, our gender, and the role appropriate to our male- or femaleness. Psychosexual development is a complex and subtle process, fraught with hazards as the human moves from infancy through childhood and adolescence to adulthood. All humans have sexual drives and, because they are social animals, sexual behaviour is shaped and controlled very largely by the society and environment into which the child is born.

Different ages and different societies evolved different patterns of behaviour. Brides of 12 and 13 were not at all uncommon in mediaeval Britain; and, indeed, in India up to the laws of 1976! What we would term 'the adolescence phase' was thus missing. In contrast it was once said of the English public-school boarding system that this was especially devised by the British to ensure late puberty and delay growing up to allow more time and energy for the examinations that must be passed for a career. Romantic pursuits and 'falling in love' were socially acceptable only after they had left school aged 18 or 19. Homosexual activity among these schoolboys may have been widespread but it has never had in our society the social approval it had in Ancient Greece.

We learn that the behaviour of the Greeks as far as love was concerned was illustrated by the saying, 'Women for business, boys for pleasure.' This is perhaps best illustrated by the Theban Band. This male-dominated society expected its men to develop their strongest love bond between each other, and the Theban Band was recognized throughout all Greece to have developed the strongest bonds of all. This warrior group consisted of 150 partnerships between older men and adolescent boys. The companionship of arms, the protectiveness of older for younger, the enjoyment of shared pleasures such as drink and song, and the ecstasies of sex, all combined to make each homosexual partnership of outstanding strength. The accumulation of 150 warrior pairs constantly exercising the pursuit of warfare with each other, and against other city states, gave Thebes the most highly trained army nucleus in all Greece. This was recognized by Alexander the Great, for when he marched against Thebes he gave orders that the Theban Band must be totally wiped out lest any survivors trained others to form a group against him. The Turks recognized the same features. For many centuries they forcibly removed the first male offspring of each Christian family, and had them brought up by older soldiers to form janissaries, a prominent corps of homosexual warriors feared throughout the Balkans.

Monogamy (one spouse at a time) is just one form of marital arrangement: other societies, with a traditional surplus of women, favour polygamy. More rare is the society where a wife has more than one legal husband at a time. Some societies encourage sexual play and imitation in their children; ours does not. Some societies look with indulgence at pre-marital sexual relations, while in other countries families are dishonoured if a daughter does not reach her husband as an intact virgin.

In Victorian England it was very rare for the elderly either to express or enjoy deep feelings attached to love and intercourse. Lord Palmerston, said to be still pursuing and seducing women at the age of 70+, was a notable exception. Only recently has society begun to recognize once more the

17

need of the elderly for deep love between themselves, and that there is no upper age limit to the capacity for enjoyable and climactic physical intercourse (Kinsey and his successors).

Humans, then, are capable of learning an almost infinite variety of patterns of sexual behaviour. In our present-day society psycho-sexual development commonly goes something like this. The baby finds it comfortable, warm and safe to be cuddled. By his reactions he can encourage his mother to prolong this body contact. The small child displays much curiosity about his body, and gets satisfaction and pleasure from playing with his genitals. The attitude of those closest to him, usually parents, largely determines his own attitude. By the time he starts school he has asked a lot of question, and begun role-playing and learning games with other children ('mothers and fathers', 'doctors and nurses'). The junior schoolchild enters a period where unity and identification with those of the same sex becomes important. He plays primarily with similarly sexed peers and shares in their sexual experiences. He develops a realistic role-definition for himself as a male. In puberty secondary sexual characteristics begin to develop and there is an uncertain interest in the opposite sex, with frequent retreats to all-boy peer groups. Adolescence is a state of very rapid growth, physical, psychological, intellectual and emotional. He will experiment sexually to gain satisfaction by masturbating alone, or with his peers, and by increasing heterosexual contacts. Adulthood is characterized by the ability to establish and maintain stable social and sexual relationships, culminating in marriage and parenthood.

We know that this development can be distorted as children learn from the attitude of their parents that sex is something dirty or not 'nice'. Henry Williamson's hero, Phillip, learns the lesson painfully:[1]

> Letting himself into the house with his latchkey, quietly, [Phillip's father] had heard the children playing in the front room; and looking round the half-open door, to give them a surprise, he had been shocked by what he had seen. There was Phillip under the table, struggling with Mavis and interfering with her clothes. Dickie heard

Phillip saying, 'Come on, be fair, I have shown you mine,
Now you must show me yours!' Hauling him in a rage
from under the table by a leg, Richard had set the boy on
his feet, and demanded to know what he meant by it.
'Nothing, Father.'
'I'll teach you to behave like that, you disgusting little
beast! How dare you?' He had shaken Phillip, hit him with
his flat hand on the side of his head, then put him across his
knee, and holding him with one hand by the neck, beaten
him as hard as he could with his other hand. Afterwards,
Phillip had been sent upstairs to bed.

Boys need to identify with the masculinity and strength of
their fathers (or a significant male figure), and girls with the
femininity of their mothers. A boy with a weak, ineffectual
father and a mother seen as a powerful and authoritative
figure may have great difficulty in achieving a mature sexual
role. The opening lines of *Portnoy's Complaint* are perhaps
the epitome of this feeling: 'She was so deeply imbedded in
my consciousness that for the first year of school I seemed to
have believed that each of my teachers was my mother in
disguise.'[2] Life (and therefore literature) has many examples
of fathers who cast a blight over their sons' development,
mothers who cling tenaciously to their daughters and thwart
all attempts at independence.

We know that some environments can cripple an individual's capacity to love. It was a common finding among
writers and researchers of the 1940s that institutionally
reared children failed to develop much love either for each
other or for their offspring.[3] These mentally deprived and
often physically stunted adolescents might freely copulate
to their own and others' climactic satisfaction but were often
uninterested in what they produced or with whom it was
shared. It seems that under bad environmental conditions,
including lack of food, humans, like animals, desert their
young, apparently without compunction if this is what they
are used to. Upbringing may teach the child to develop the
capacity to love, in the sense of depth of feeling for another
human, but he goes on learning from his life experiences. If
his social world disintegrates through war, famine, or nothing

19

more dramatic than a series of episodes of being hurt and let down by other humans, it is highly probable his behaviour will become more and more centred on his own needs, and less and less on those of any other. Divorce is an example.

We may seem to have strayed rather far from our subject, but it is against this complex background that we must look at the psycho-sexual development of the mentally handicapped in our society. What commonly happens to them? We have seen that normal children become socialized through interactions with parents, peer groups and school, and share the sexual experiences of their age group away from adult eyes. By contrast, the mentally handicapped child is born to a sheltered environment, for it is expected that he will remain dependent in some way all his life. Often his sexual nature is denied by those who care for him, right from his earliest years. As he grows he becomes aware of sexuality in many of the ways normal children do – TV, cinema, gossip, observation – but unlike the normal child his social activity is closely supervised and sexual expressions of behaviour are often discouraged. His psycho-sexual development can become distorted because of the attitudes and misconceptions of the people around him. Many mentally handicapped people are embarrassed by their bodies. As children they are often over-corrected as they show natural curiosity about themselves, and ever afterwards feel guilty and uneasy looking in bathroom mirrors or at pictures. Roland, for example, a mentally handicapped lad of 19, wandered into the room where we were reviewing films for this book. On the screen was a slide showing a man dressed in shorts and plimsolls doing a knees-bend exercise. 'Dirty,' giggled Roland. We were somewhat puzzled (the slide was ancient and the shorts were voluminous!). 'What's dirty, Roland?' 'Showing his tits. Dirty.' Roland had never had any formal health or sex education, but from somewhere he had acquired a decidedly negative attitude towards certain parts of the body. The normal child gradually acquires 'ownership' of his body. When he is small, care of his body is in the control of his mother (or her substitute) and is handed over slowly as the child grows up. Various parts are handed over at different times, and the private parts of the body (genitals) are among the last to be the responsibility of the youngster. For a long time he may have the feeling his penis does not really belong to him, it is something apart. Then quite suddenly he may be expected to 'own' his own genitals and use them with confidence.[4]

The mentally handicapped person may never be allowed to 'own' even the non-sexual parts of his body – one more area of difficulty in relating to himself and his sexuality.

The mentally handicapped individual raised in an institution has additional difficulties. The adults surrounding him are often emotionally neutral to each other, so there are no loving relationships on which to base his own adult behaviour. In the recent past nearly all institutions were either mono-sexual, or the males and females were firmly segregated. Once more, there was very little opportunity for normal learning. Sexual expression was of necessity directed towards accessible fellow-patients and was thus homosexual. Lack of privacy and lack of training meant also that masturbation was a highly visible 'problem'. It is by no means easy to provide a residential environment where adolescents can develop normally. As Peter Righton of the National Institute for Social Work points out:[5]

> Adolescents living with their families value very highly the opportunity to gain emotional and sexual experience through freely-chosen relationships outside the home. If the opportunity is not granted to them as a right, most will either fight to acquire it or pursue their friendships clandestinely; in either case, many find ingenious ways of circumventing parental prohibition and disapproval. In residential care there are almost always overwhelming pressures on staff, from actual or presumed public opinion, to exercise vigilant control over the quantity and quality of interaction between adolescent residents and the neighbourhood. As a consequence, the outside encounters (spiced with at least the possibility of sexual adventure) that most young people take for granted tend, with varying degrees of subtlety, to be comparatively restricted,

supervised and 'policed' for adolescents in residential units. It is not seldom that such encounters are – in effect, if not overtly – forbidden altogether.

He goes on:

> what really carries the risk of deprivation for people in residential care is not so much the panics and prohibitions, the distress and embarrassment that often surround the act of sex itself. It is rather their insidious extension to the expression of those emotions which are commonly the precursors of sex – tenderness, affection and warmth expressed through touch. Opportunities for loving interchange are needs as fundamental to human beings as are sun and water to plants, and these needs are specially urgent for all categories of resident, who commonly suffer from double deprivation – first, the handicap or disadvantageous life circumstances which preceded their admission to care; secondly the very fact of being in care at all.

Different people have different reactions to expressions of sexual behaviour, reactions which stem from past personal experiences. Some staff feel very strongly that masturbation and homosexual behaviour are wrong and harmful and will over-react to what they see going on around them. Others may turn a blind eye to that but feel very concerned that a pregnancy would give the unit a bad reputation. One reacts against solitary or homosexual activity, another against heterosexual activities. No wonder the mentally handicapped get confused and grow up with negative attitudes towards their bodies. Anything they do is always bound to be wrong according to somebody. Indeed, the whole subject of touch, sexuality and power in residential establishments is largely ignored – an oversight which causes much confusion, unhappiness and tension in residents and care staff alike.[6]

A recent survey of staff in American institutions for the mentally handicapped showed in the author's words, that 'a commitment to principles of normalisation encounters severe strains in the area of sexual behaviour'.[7] The survey is worth looking at because although there has been no comparable research in Britain it is probable that results would be much the same. Responses to a questionnaire were received from sixty-nine residential units. Seventy per cent of respondents would welcome a delineated set of guide lines on the best way to handle sexual behaviour of residents, but only 23 per cent of the units had such written policies. Not surprisingly there were marked discrepancies between the specific sexual behaviours which occurred, those which were permitted, and those the respondents felt ought to have been allowed. Finally, while 67 per cent of the respondents felt that sexual frustration contributed to a significant or major degree to most mentally handicapped people's problems of adjustment, the only forms of sexual relief that a majority thought ought to be permitted were private masturbation, brief public and private kissing, and private heterosexual petting. Thus, although there was a clear recognition of the problem of sexual frustration, there was hesitancy in allowing any solution.

Can anything be done to correct distortions in psycho-sexual development, to alter socially aberrant behaviour where the mentally handicapped are concerned?

First, we must not underestimate the remarkable human capacity for change and adaptation. When living conditions become more normal, so often, too, does behaviour. In 1971 a newly built North Wales hospital received 300 in-patients from old mono-sexual hospitals due to close. In the new mixed hospital wards some middle-aged, even elderly men, previously cared for in mono-sexual institutions and accepted as confirmed homosexuals, turned to the opposite sex with so little reluctance, so much enthusiasm, and developed such skills, that one of the authors found himself rebuking a 67 year old 'homosexual' for playing off three of his girl friends against each other.

There are others, of course, who do not change the direction of their sexual interests quite so readily. They may need more help and structured learning. In an interesting article, Rosen describes some of the techniques that could be used in programmes which would channel sexual responsiveness.[8]

One such technique is *desensitization*. The prospect of contacts with members of the opposite sex can be very frightening to those who have lacked opportunities to acquire the social skills necessary. Anxiety-producing situations are

23

graded in intensity, and by linking these to deep-muscle relaxation sessions the subject is aided to gradually overcome his fear. After this the individual can practise in *programmed heterosexual experiences*, a series of planned exercises, progressing from just seeing a female therapist in the distance, to talking briefly to her, engaging her in conversation, etc. The subject will eventually be ready to try out the same learned behaviour in real situations. *Role playing* can be helpful in increasing the social skills necessary for successful interpersonal relationships. Responses for a variety of situations can be practised with the therapist until the subject feels more confident and less worried.

The misconceptions and distortions in the sexual knowledge that the mentally handicapped individual possesses means that frank *talk about sex* with a therapist may serve to reduce anxiety. Rosen also found a surprising absence of *masturbatory activity* among boys with deviant sexual behaviour. There was some progress in substituting masturbation for the inappropriate behaviour. *Aversive-conditioning* techniques may be used when subjects have developed bizarre or perverted sexual behaviour.

In talking about techniques for enhancing the social skills necessary for heterosexual relationships and correcting inappropriate sexual behaviour, we must not overlook a vital point. In the words of Jean Vanier, founder of the L'Arche sheltered communities, the search of the mentally handicapped:[9]

> like anyone else's, is not simply for sexual gratification but for the far deeper experience of love – for the assurance that they are a person, and a loveable person, and a person who can give love. An active sexual life no more brings this assurance to a mentally handicapped person than it does anyone else; without growth in friendship, tenderness and fidelity, sexual activity is no more than a caricature of love.

With some humans love, like trust, must be re-learnt; it can greatly enrich the quality of life to be lived. True, there are risks involved – loving and being hurt, trusting and being deceived, sharing hopes and dreams and having them shattered. These are risks for us all, whatever our handicaps. Yet humans need humans, risks pay off, people respond to those that need them, form stable partnerships and gain much from each other in terms of emotional and physical comfort. The experience of loving someone with as many or more difficulties as oneself can often stimulate able-bodied and handicapped persons alike. Caring deeply about what happens to another human can bring out untapped strengths, and the partnerships formed give a stability and maturity which singly the partners lack.

With counselling and support, the handicapped can be aided in this, as in other matters, to help themselves. That, we think, is a very worth-while goal.

4 The problems of adolescence

In this chapter we shall look at the problems of mentally handicapped and dull normal teenagers. The adolescent period is most likely to have crises of behaviour, bewildering to parent and teenager alike. The years between childhood and adulthood seldom pass peacefully, whether the teenager is intellectually handicapped or not. We have only to recall the statistics on schoolgirl pregnancies, adolescent crime-rates and deaths due to motor-cycle accidents, to remind ourselves it is a time of testing for all concerned.

We have put together a case history which, to preserve anonymity, is an amalgam of several. Sally does not exist but we think she is not far from reality. We have made it the story of a teenage girl rather than boy, because even in these days of supposed sexual equality, female promiscuity is condemned while, in the main, male promiscuity is condoned or at least not viewed so seriously. In the first section, we shall be looking at things from Sally's point of view. What was it like to be on the receiving end of the care system? Did it help or hinder maturity? Is it possible to relearn a more socially acceptable attitude towards sexuality? In the second section we shall shift our stance and look through the eyes of the adults involved – Sally's family, and the care staff whom she frequently made to feel angry, inadequate and helpless. Were chances missed? How does society cope with a promiscuous youngster who craves affection and has learnt to use (or abuse) her body to obtain love, money or attention? In the final part we look at the dilemmas facing loving and concerned parents.

A young person's view: Sally's story

Sally's conception was one of those 'mistakes' which sometimes happens when a woman thinks her family is complete. Her mother railed against fate, but her father was captivated by his new daughter's rather fey, otherworldly, look, not uncommon in children of older parents. Sally was very much a 'Daddy's girl' and when, at the age of 4, her parents divorced, she missed him greatly. She became a clinging child, began to wet her bed, and constantly came off worst in any competition with her older and rougher siblings. She hated school and took refuge in a make-believe world of her own. By the time Sally was 12 all her brothers and sisters had moved on and she was left alone with her mother. She liked this but was very demanding and in fact was very immature. Her school work had also suffered and she was placed in the remedial class at the local school. Her IQ test gave a result of 68, thought to be 'optimistic'. All went reasonably well for a year or so until her mother's lover moved into the house. Sally had few real memories of her own father, but bitterly resented a new addition to the household as once again she took second place in her mother's affections. She began to get into trouble outside and had several court appearances. Inevitably the situation exploded. Sally later wrote her side of the story:

> My mum and her fancy man got drunk one night. Well I went straight up to bed and I heard them start shouting and calling each other awful names. Mum ran upstairs and shut herself in and Uncle Jim broke something. Everything went quiet and I went to sleep. I woke up when the door of my bedroom opened and I was just going to shout 'Mum' when he said, 'It's only me, I'm coming in with

you.' I told him 'No' but he got in anyway and did something to me. I cried afterwards and he told me to shut up and he went out. Next morning my mother said I'd been dreaming and I cried again. She said if I didn't forget what I'd told her she would put me away. Well I was in a temper and I smashed my cup and the plate on the floor. I ran out of the door and across the road, a man in a car shouted at me but I didn't stop and I ran all the way to my probation officer.

Sally was put in a children's home for a week, then at a court hearing she was placed in the care of the local authority. She could not settle in any of the places tried. Basically she missed her mother, her own home and resented sharing attention with the other children. She ran away.

It was like a game, the further you got the longer you had by yourself with the person who took you back. It was the only time you could really talk to them. I used to hitch rides in all kinds of lorries, I met lots of men and I really got into the way of it. It was easy to get a bit of money – sometimes you only had to threaten and they paid up.

At 14 she set fire to rubbish in a wastepaper basket with a cigarette, and was sent to the more secure environment of a remand home while the authorities drew breath and took stock. Her abscons ions had meant that her schooling was at best intermittent, and this, together with her known dullness, led the authorities to try the resources of the local mental-handicap hospital. For a year this was a successful placement. At the beginning she was in a locked ward, which gave everybody security and she formed good relationships with the staff, who found her appealing and brighter than most.

I went to school there. The teacher was very nice. I done different things than the other children because what they done was simple things. Well I went every day to school, and to the pictures they showed, and dances and had my hair done for free. I thought now I am really happy but after a time I got fed up.

After a year Sally was discharged from the hospital into the care of one of her married sisters, as her mother did not want anything to do with her. She acquired a job and a boy friend, both of which lasted only a few weeks as she was insolent to the work supervisor and flirted outrageously with the boy's best friend. She was unsettled and bored and began to make overtures to her sister's husband. The family temper had passed to both sisters and in the row which followed they had to be separated by the neighbours.

Sally was still officially in the care of the local authority, so she went to a working girls' hostel. There, something always went wrong with the jobs she tried. She took cigarettes and sweets: 'Well, they didn't pay me enough.' The social worker went back to mother. Sally had not seen her for three years, and this time gap had helped to heal the bitterness with which they had parted. In court Sally's mother offered to give her a chance and have her home again. Uncle Jim was still on the scene. Sally's very good looks and large, deep-blue eyes made her a very attractive young woman. Her mother soon regretted her gesture of good will.

One day Mum said something funny to me, and me and Jim looked at each other and started to laugh. Well, Mum threw her cup on the floor and said, 'There's something going on between you and him.' But of course there was nothing because I hated him after what he had done to me, I'd never forgive him. My mother wouldn't listen and I lost my temper. I was fed up with her keeping an eye on me, do this, do that all the time and her thinking I'd want that man. I ran away that night.

Still 'in care', she was sent to a remand home. There her tested IQ was found to have risen to 90 – it seemed her enforced stay in hospital had enabled her to catch up on her education. Until a new place was found she was supposed to stay in the home. She managed to abscond twice, once from an escorted walk, the next time through a window and up over the very tall gate. On the second occasion she was away for a month and was brought back by three policemen, all four looking the worse for wear as Sally had screamed and scratched for the whole of the 10 mile journey. She claimed she had been living with a man who had picked her up and that she was pregnant by him:

'Now I'll have someone to care for, it'll give me a sense of responsibility.'

But her hopes in this direction were unfounded. She broke crockery, scratched and tore, and her disturbed behaviour led the authorities once again to approach a psychiatric hospital, and Sally found herself in a locked ward, detained compulsorily for a month. This time, however, she bitterly resented the label 'mentally disordered', and indeed she had little in common with the other residents. She felt herself misplaced, and desperately wanted to prove she was an adult who not only could care for herself but for a child as well. She caused the staff much heart-searching as she refused to take the prescribed birth-control pill and announced her intention of becoming pregnant at the first opportunity. The male staff began to wear a hunted look; the female nurses reacted uncertainly as they debated the ethics of protecting a woman against herself. Fortunately the situation never came to a head – there were one or two false alarms but over the month Sally's frantic mood calmed and her seventeenth birthday brought her nearer the maturity she wished to command. She formed a close relationship with a motherly nurse who had two teenage daughters of her own and who had the gift of seeing through Sally's rude talk and bravado to the needful, uncertain and unhappy girl beneath. Her detaining section expired and she agreed to remain informally for a while.

Sally's mother came to see her and although the meeting was restrained on both sides it went sufficiently well for her mother to ask if she would like to spend a weekend at home. Sally was pleased by the invitation and it was arranged to coincide with a visit of one of her brothers and his family. Sally enjoyed playing with her young niece and nephew, but was not so pleased when the baby was sick over her newly washed hair. Her mother's house was small, and it was all a bit of a squeeze. On her return Sally confided to the nurse that she thought babies were rather overrated.

Her visits home continued, although at a case conference both Sally and her mother said they thought too much had passed between them for her ever to live permanently at home again. The fact that they smiled ruefully at each other as they spoke, suggested that Sally saw this not as yet another rejection, but as a passing to a new stage in her life. It was agreed that residence in a hospital was inappropriate and that her social worker would try to find placement in lodgings with a sympathetic person who would be part foster mother, part landlady. Case conferences usually tend towards optimistic recommendations, but in this instance the social worker was fortunate enough to locate a couple who ran a bed and breakfast boarding-house and whose youngest daughter had just got married. Sally met them and liked them, she was on her best behaviour and they felt she had been hard done by in her short life.

The honeymoon period lasted three weeks, then Sally began to test the limits of her freedom. She stayed out late, refused to get up on time, played her transistor at full volume, and drifted around the house in a nightie which revealed more than it hid. Not surprisingly, the strain began to tell on Mr and Mrs Cameron – 'Our daughters were never like this' – and in spite of intensive social-work support a crisis seemed imminent. Fate, however, played an unexpected hand. Mr Cameron had a serious heart attack which for a while left Mrs Cameron single-handed to carry on the boarding-house on which their income depended. Of their own children one was now in Canada and the other two had young children of their own. There was only Sally to depend on for regular help. No one had needed Sally in a way that was meaningful to her before. She felt she had always taken second place in her mother's affections, first to her brothers and sisters, then with Jim. Her various lovers were almost all birds of passage who had used and abused her, and of her acquaintances she once said sadly, 'The friends that I've got I don't like.' Faced with an obvious need and appeal for her help she responded cheerfully and with enjoyment. She even roped in her current boyfriend to help with some re-decorating. The frequency of social-work visits declined and when Sally reached her eighteenth birthday and was officially free to do as she wished, she asked if she could remain with the Camerons.

What were the feelings of the various adults who played a part in Sally's story? In order to illustrate the concerns of the many people involved with an upset and difficult adolescent we now try to put their point of view.

The adult view

Sally's mother held the opinion that she had not had an easy life. Over the years her marriage had reached a stage of mutual indifference and it came as a severe blow to find herself pregnant after a gap of eight years. She blamed her husband for his carelessness and never warmed to the new baby as she had to the others. The rows became more frequent and Sally's father moved away to a quieter life with a quieter woman.

Sally missed him very much and her behaviour got on her mother's nerves. She seemed to want more attention than all the others put together and was constantly whining when things did not go her way. When the older children grew up and left home and Sally had her mother to herself she grew less insistent, and her behaviour caused less irritation. She was company for her mother and they got on quite well together. Although Mrs West had not been particularly happy in her marriage, she found time hanging rather heavily and she missed a male figure about the house. She had enough distrust not to want to marry again, but she did not see why she should lead a life of celibacy. Jim was not much of a catch, but he did keep her warm at nights, and his extra money was useful. It should have been a comfortable arrangement, for she felt she could manage him.

Unfortunately Sally was the nigger in the wood pile and all Mrs West's resentment flared up again. When Sally began thieving from local shops Mrs West felt shamed and her daughter's active dislike of Jim filled the home atmosphere with tension. There was no denying that Sally was a physically attractive child and although she had benefited little from her formal schooling she was precocious in her knowledge of the more smutty aspects of the facts of life. She used her large blue eyes to great advantage.

Mrs West did not know whether or not to believe Sally's accusation that Jim had interfered with her. She knew that Jim thought Sally needed some sort of lesson, she knew he had been drinking that evening, and she knew she had locked her own bedroom door. She was afraid of what the truth might mean; it was easier to deny the whole thing. She backed up Jim's story but heaved a sigh of relief when she was not believed and Sally was removed from the house.

The staff at the various children's homes felt themselves stretched to their limits by Sally. She could be so bright, charming and helpful on her good days, but all too often was sulky, spiteful and deliberately dense. She soon learned that the best way to get the attention she craved was to run away – there was always a talk with the Warden on return, and a certain notoriety among the other children. The staffing ratios were never generous, and much of their time was spent in caring for the physical needs of the 14–20 children in each of the homes that attempted to help Sally. It is a familiar story – either wardens, staff or children came and went, nothing was settled, nothing was permanent. None of Sally's brothers or sisters was in a position to offer help and although at first the idea of a foster home was mooted, Sally's tendency to run away made it difficult to proceed. Staff were upset by Sally's precocious behaviour and her outrageous stories of how she lived while on the run. They felt, not unnaturally, she was a bad influence on the other youngsters. The episode when Sally set fire to a wastepaper basket in the bedroom 'to test the new sprinkler system' was the last straw, and the straw which was used to pass Sally on to a new phase in her care.

Placement in the secure environment of a locked ward in a subnormality hospital sounds a drastic step, but the idea of the hospital as an 'asylum' is an ancient one. Sally needed an enforced respite from the pattern of life she was slipping into. She needed time to take stock and catch up not only on formal schooling but with the normal pursuits of 14 year old girls. From the first she spent more time in the company of staff than other residents. She became a favourite, behaving well because she got lots of warm-hearted attention and was treated as being more responsible than the others. In nearly all ways it was one of the happiest years Sally had known. Of course, a secure, caring environment does not have to be in a mental-handicap hospital.

Both hospital and social workers were concerned that Sally stayed no longer than she need, especially as her teacher's reports spoke of her developing abilities. Sally's eldest sister offered her the chance of a new home in a new area and all hoped this would be a new start. Unfortunately she did not fully appreciate how difficult this rather unknown kid sister would be to handle. Thinking herself free at last of all restraints Sally did not see why she should put with a dull factory job or a dull social life. Her sister quickly repented of her generosity when her own husband was threatened by Sally's siren act.

Social workers hoped Sally was ready for the more adult setting of a working girls' hostel. But although people tried hard to settle her in a job Sally hated routine and always found excuses to explain why she could not possibly have stayed another week. The usual one was that the men could not keep their hands to themselves, but it was likely that Sally had started it all by relieving monotony in her own way. She committed some particularly obvious thefts but was given a conditional discharge when Mrs West appeared in court to offer Sally another chance at home.

With the benefit of hindsight it is obvious this had little likelihood of success – the intervening period had turned Sally from a pretty, appealing child, to a young woman of undoubted attractiveness, while her mother was three years older and feeling it. Mrs West helped her find a job to get her out of the house and was cross when Sally decided it was all too much like hard work and walked out after only a fortnight. She tried to ensure Sally was home in the evenings at a reasonable hour, but Sally had no intention of curtailing her enjoyment or of knuckling under to discipline, especially when Jim tried to back her mother up. They all began to look askance at each other and it did not take long for the flare-up to come.

There was much professional debate as to Sally's placement. At first sight, admission to a psychiatric hospital seems a drastic step, but it was undeniable that the girl was disturbed and needed psychiatric help. On the one hand the staff sympathized with the predicament Sally found herself in, on the other they felt professionally threatened as she refused medical advice and disrupted ward routine. Are nurses within their rights to force an in-patient to take prescribed medication, in this case the birth-control pill? How hard should they work to persuade someone it is in their best interests to do so? How hard to dissuade from a course of action many normal teenagers follow? Standing in *locus parenti* is never simple, but in this case the whole hospital debated the issue without coming to any firm conclusions. One nurse particularly took Sally to her heart and encouraged her to think about the sort of future she wanted for herself. In many ways it was a new line of thought for Sally, who had not seen any further than a warm cuddly baby who would give her back the love she felt she had inside her. The nurse helped her look beyond this idyllic vision to the loneliness and hardship it would mean without a partner to share the difficulties. She listened without visible signs of shock to Sally relating her experiences. Not surprisingly the girl had little sense of her own worth as a person and confessed she had never had much pleasure from sex but it was usually a means to an end. The nurse gave her a basic, earthy woman-to-woman talk about dealing with men and not abusing her body. It seemed that none of her partners had felt genuine affection for Sally and, although she could fool herself for a while, disillusionment had always followed. She thought love stories were stupid – everyone was deluding themselves. The nurse told her that selfishness only gets selfishness back in return, and that friendship means thinking that other people and their feelings are just as important as one's own. She chatted to Sally about her own daughters, made her laugh at herself, and told her off in no uncertain terms when she was rude and intolerant. Sally liked her because she knew exactly where she stood.

After three months Sally's progress was reviewed at a case conference. She was keen to get away from the hospital and was hopeful she could start afresh – 'after all, I'm 17 now.' The ward staff were a little cynical of her airy optimism, but all agreed she had earned another chance. The social services were already running a campaign to recruit foster parents for adolescents in care and one of the couples who responded took an interest in Sally's story. They were warned that the job they were considering undertaking would be extremely demanding on their time, temper and emotions. The people who are prepared to take on such challenges form a vital part of the resources available to a society. Fostering children requires special human skills; fostering teenagers would try the patience of saints. Sally presented an especial challenge as her repertoire of responses had little in the middle range of behaviour. She was accustomed to leave no one in any doubt of her displeasure.

The Camerons tried to be both tolerant and firm, to work out with her reasonable rules, and to treat her as a responsible person. It was inevitable that Sally should test out their good intentions by reverting to all the behaviour which had previously been so successful in upsetting people. It naturally upset the Camerons and they began to feel they had bitten off more than they could chew.

Mr Cameron's illness brought Sally up short. For once in her life she forgot herself and her own feelings and did her best to help. The work was varied enough to stop her getting bored and she basked in the Camerons' praise. Fortunately they were in a position to offer her a long-term home, the only place where she had been really settled since she was 12 years old.

Could Sally have been helped more satisfactorily at an earlier stage? It is, of course, problematical. She kept people off-balance, so busy reacting to her behaviour that they found it difficult to see further than the current outrage. Her experiences taught her only the negative, destructive aspect of sexuality. She showed such detailed knowledge of the seamier side of life that no one felt it was necessary to talk to her about the wider implications of sexuality – they only spoke in prohibitory terms. She was almost 17 before she trusted someone enough to confide in them about her puzzlement and doubt about love, affection and sex. Would she have listened when she was younger? Again it is problematical, and we leave the reader to draw his own conclusions.

Parental dilemmas

We arranged Sally's case history to show many of the difficulties of a disturbed adolescence. That is one aspect of the picture. But what of the many loving and concerned parents who want to do their best for their handicapped youngster but who feel themselves faced with social and moral dilemmas at every turn? For better or worse, teenagers of normal intelligence gradually come to act with autonomy and responsibility. Parents may try to exercise some control over the friends their children choose but eventually most parents have to recognize this is a matter of personal preference. Parents do not usually expect to oversee the dating and courtship of their children, but most would expect that their children would eventually present a chosen partner to them. They do not expect to teach their normal child to masturbate, though most assume that their children will learn this. Developments usually taken for granted may never be reached by handicapped teenagers. This means that parents have consciously to make choices, and may feel uneasy that they appear to be taking the lead too much and perhaps pushing their children too far too fast along the path to adulthood.

It is by no means easy to decide whether or not to teach one's handicapped son or daughter to masturbate, but it can help to reduce the sexual tension which builds up. Parents have to be the best judge of the amount of sexual tension their teenager is experiencing. Masturbation is the normal way of reducing this tension, whether one is handicapped or not, providing it is clearly understood to be a private activity.

Many parents with a handicapped adolescent become concerned about the too rapid and too enthusiastic development of a friendship. Adolescents vary greatly in the age at which they develop close friendships with the opposite sex. Some are keen to date at the age of 12, others pass right through to the 20s without displaying any interest. Nor does the degree of handicap appear to make much difference. Some normal boys educated in public boarding schools develop their first sexual friendship in university; we have seen a 12 year old mongol girl make explicitly sexual overtures to a teacher of whom she became passionately fond.

37

The dilemma a normal parent finds him or herself in is to choose between the paths available. Most will want their daughter to have as normal a life as possible, yet wish to protect her from the dangers of enthusiastic friendship. This is particularly so when a near normal daughter wishes to join in the dances and drinking outings of her very normal friends, and keep the same late hours. Each situation must be judged on its own merits. Our advice is for the parent to seek the help of the teacher, trainer, social worker or doctor who is most sympathetic and most knowledgeable about a particular situation emerging. It must be recognized that for personal reasons some of these professionals become very upset at discussing sexual development. However, there is usually a choice among the professional advisers and it is best for both parents to go to the one who appears most helpful. It is for this purpose that we describe in detail in chapter 8 the development of a sex-education programme to meet the needs of the different levels of handicapped young people. The parents may feel unhappy handling this subject themselves. If so, professionals involved in the day care can give the teenager individual or group guidance.

How far should friendships be encouraged without the parents feeling they are contriving a social life for their children? Most special schools and adult training centres have social clubs which meet once a week. Just as with normal adolescents, the parents can often play a highly constructive part by providing transport at appropriate times. Where dances, parties and other outings are in question, even normal adolescents are often quite appreciative of a parent driving them to and back from an evening excursion. In the early teenage years normal youngsters usually go out together in mixed groups, and handicapped teenagers can invite in some friends for a record session or an evening of simple card and table games. If parents can withdraw to another room for a time so much the better. It will probably be necessary to discuss rules of behaviour, as often mentally handicapped teenagers are uncertain about things like how loud the record player ought to be, how much they should eat, what time they should go home.

Where a handicapped youngster shows a special preference

for a friend of the opposite sex, parents are again faced with a decision – should this be encouraged or not? If the feeling is returned we think there is much to be gained from such a friendship. Of course there is risk involved, risk that one's son or daughter will be hurt, but being hurt is as much part of being human as loving, caring and sharing. Again, 'rules' of conduct will probably need to be clearly spelled out. Remember, mentally handicapped teenagers often do not have the finance, independence of movement or social ability to exploit the possibilities normal teenagers embark upon. If they meet only at home they will be highly visible; it is not fair to tell them off for cuddling each other when the family is present, and not to allow them some privacy. Teenagers often talk in extremes, and if the girl says she loves and adores her current boy friend, it does not necessarily mean that she wishes to leap into bed with him at once – she is probably just using the only words she knows to to describe a feeling she has not had before. If she, like many others before her, weeps bitterly when her boy fails to telephone, it may well be that he has merely lost the number – or does not know how to phone it. The giving and receiving of presents is a tricky social art, for while small gifts may comfort, large ones can embarrass. To show the depth of affection felt the mentally handicapped youngster may overdo generosity, and again it is best for parents to discuss limits and set a financial ceiling.

Finally, most parents will want to review the possibilities of contraception. The objection often raised is that expecting it to be necessary will only encourage the teenager to act irresponsibly. But surely it is far better to acknowledge that, like everyone else, they will be subject to temptation and, like everyone else, may not always resist it as hard as they might. It is not a question of trusting or not trusting, but of taking normal, sensible precautions.

Contraception

Professional medical advice is quite essential. Despite newspaper reports, there are few side effects with the latest oral contraceptive preparations and for advice on these the parent is best guided by the family doctor. Contraception is most likely to be needed with the near normal girl who insists on behaving even more 'normally' than her friends. Since risks run are so much tied up with the life style of the adolescent concerned and how much he or she insists, or is able, to move around the community unaccompanied, then this is very much an area in which professional guidance must be sought. Most girls at risk accept the advice of their elders in avoiding a pregnancy that may be devastatingly unhappy, although just as some normal adolescents try to use pregnancy as a solution to a severe personal need, the mentally handicapped adolescent girl who says she wants a 'living doll' is best taken by the parent to a professional adviser.

Apart from the daily 'Pill', which is likely to contain variable quantities of the hormones oestrogen or progesterone, according to the preparation the doctor advises, there are now monthly injections available which place within the body a depot of the drug to last four weeks. In addition there is the intrauterine device which has to be fitted by a specialist in this procedure at a clinic or hospital and lasts for some three years. Due to the risk of contamination or unexpected slippage there should be an annual medical check-up, although such devices have been known to stay in place for up to six years without attention or trouble.

Sterilization

Often a request for this is made in response to a fear rather than to an actual situation. Or if a situation does exist, i.e. the girl is promiscuous or is being used sexually, sterilization will not 'solve' that particular problem; and there are other ways of preventing unwanted pregnancy.

In our experience sterilization is rarely, if ever, required during adolescence. For the reasons given in this book it is seldom indicated on the grounds that the mother will give birth to a genetically misendowed child. Almost always the adolescent at risk under the age of 16 is best advised to be on the Pill, have an injection or an intrauterine device. The girl in her late teens who knowingly places herself at risk, may either be of a rising ability level so that in ten years' time she may wish to marry, settle down and have a child, or else may have personal difficulties and need professional advice. In many years of professional practice neither of us has ever had to be a party to the sterilization of a minor. There have always been better ways of handling these problems.

Conclusion

True, Sally does not exist, but there are many who would recognize something of their own lives in her story. We have portrayed her as extremely self-centred and selfish, a common enough characteristic of adolescents. Mentally handicapped youngsters may be even more insensitive to the needs and feelings of other people, for they are often unable to imagine themselves in someone else's shoes. They simply do not appreciate the hurt they sometimes cause in pursuit of their own satisfaction, whether to their contemporaries, parents or care staff. Much patience will be needed, especially as the difficulties of adolescence may span a longer period of time than is usual with normal youngsters.

It is easy for things to get out of proportion, particularly if the mentally handicapped teenager is an only child. Informal discussion groups, meeting perhaps in a different home once a fortnight or so, can be extremely helpful. Parents can then have a chance to air anxieties, compare notes, and offer and receive advice and support. Your local branch of the National Society for Mentally Handicapped Children, or local social workers, may help to start something like this.

Adolescence is often a turbulent period, but with patience, counselling and a sense of humour, all should come through!

5 Love and the mentally handicapped

> 'It is best to love wisely, no doubt; but to love
> foolishly is better than not to be able to love at all.'
> Thackeray, *Pendennis*

Can the mentally handicapped love like other people? Do they experience the depth of feeling we associate with falling in love? No research programme can quantify the amount of love one person feels for another; the mixture of emotion, commitment, self-interest and self-denial is indeed a tangled web.

We know that behaviour is conditioned by life experiences and we know that many mentally handicapped people lead socially abnormal lives, brought up in large groups, with ever-changing authority figures. Others are over-protected by parents. So what are their chances of loving wisely, or foolishly, of forming strong bonds of attachment? How far does intelligence play a part in this? We would say that it plays very little, for it is a human capacity to give and receive love, and being a severely handicapped mongol with 47 instead of 46 chromosomes, or having an IQ well below average, does not seem to alter this need. But it is worth restating the point: the way we love, the way we behave towards the person we love, largely follows from what we have experienced in the past. A few case histories illustrate this point.[1]

Barry

Barry was an institutionally reared mongol boy. Abandoned by his parents when young, he was raised in a ward of forty handicapped boys and staffed for most of his childhood by no more than two nurses at any one time. The work was hard and many nurses came and went over the years. Barry, now 20, is a cheerful, mischievous, pleasant man, talkative, happy to go with anybody, who thoroughly enjoys hopping into bed to make love with anybody who wants him, but who will steal anything that takes his fancy and laugh uproariously when he is found out. Shifting attention and affection rapidly and shallowly from one person to another is the perfect example of an institutionally reared human who has no deep feeling for anybody and who shares his life with all. Fortunately, as he still lives in an institution, he will never be convicted for the theft, burglary, homosexuality or blackmail that he practises, for all clearly recognize that he practises what he has been taught. He has learnt all too well.

Betty

Betty, a petite and sweet-natured mentally handicapped woman, was swept off her feet by a strong and exciting young man, Paul, some fifteen years her junior. He had been treated for personality disorder, and although he loves her probably as much as he has loved anyone, he is not the most considerate of husbands. Betty has been hurt many times by his callousness and lack of thought. But having made her choice, she sticks by him. What is more important than anything is the fact she now has her own place and status in the world: '[Marriage] has brought me out more. Given me another chance in the world, because I've been in Homes all over. I'm more happier now, it's nice to come in here and open the door on my own home.' She is proud of Paul when he has done nothing to warrant praise, loves him when others are finding him most trying. We are reminded of Bertrand Russell's comment (*The Conquest of Happiness*): 'Many people when they fall in love look for a little haven of refuge from the world, where they can be sure of being admired when they are not admirable, and praised when they are not praiseworthy.'

Linda

Linda is not married at the time of writing, although she very much hopes to be soon. She does not rate very high on the IQ scale (55) but she has a lot of other things going for her. She is young, vivacious and pretty. She is also kind-hearted, and some would say this has been her undoing. She has had one baby and numerous boy friends. Last year she met in her hostel a rather quiet young man. They began to go out together and then there was talk of marriage. It might be thought that Linda, usually a happy-go-lucky soul not noted for her forethought, would not be very worried about her future, but this is not so. Her fiancé, Tom, is epileptic and although normally well controlled by medication, since Linda entered his life stresses have increased and so have his fits. One of Linda's former boy friends hovers threateningly in the background and both know he is quite capable of violence. Where, Linda wonders, can they live that will be safe? She is worried, too, about Tom's fits and if she will be able to cope with them. What should she do when he falls to the floor? Will he be calmer after marriage? They have been courting for a year and Linda, with her greater experience, is mothering Tom as best she can. Now that she has found someone with whom she wishes to settle down she has matured in her behaviour. She even goes so far as to write to us: 'I am [the] tipe that wor[r]y a lot.' Two years ago no one would have recognized that description of Linda. But she has changed. She has much to give the shy and diffident Tom and their partnership might be expected to be of benefit to them both.[2]

Bill and Ida

We tell the story of Bill and Ida in chapter 6. They are both severely subnormal. To watch them together it would be hard indeed to deny that the mentally handicapped have the same capacity to love as the rest of mankind. They remembered each other during long years of separation and were absolutely delighted at their reunion. They give each other much comfort and affection and are happy and content with their lot. Each has what most people would settle for – a truly loving partner, a comfortable home, stable employment and income, and freedom to please themselves about how they spend their leisure hours.

Nell and Luke

Of course not all are so fortunate as Bill and Ida. Reading Nell's case history it is not difficult to see why she finds it so hard to love anyone, even herself. This dull, unlovely child was rejected and abandoned by one relative after another. She grew into a miserable and moody young woman, never finding satisfaction in any friendship or relationship. Somewhat surprisingly one young man latched on to her and claimed her as his own. Luke desperately needed someone to belong to and someone who would belong to him. His childhood had been equally disastrous to his ability to love. Both parents were schizophrenic and his care was erratic and affectionless. When still quite small he witnessed the siege and invasion of his home by mental welfare officers, aided by the police, as his father waved a shotgun in all directions. Luke was perhaps still young enough to recover from his damaged start in life, but a further misfortune befell him. The children's unit to which he went was well organized and appeared to provide a good substitute home. But within a year or two it broke up when the warden was charged with seducing the children – Luke included. All were dispersed to different homes.

Luke yearned for stability and tenaciously courted Nell, despite frequent and cruel rejections by her. She blew cold much more often than she blew hot. Why did he persist, when it was perfectly obvious to everyone else, other residents as well as staff, that he was banging his head against a brick wall? Being mildly schizophrenic Luke's grasp of reality is not always one hundred per cent, and his mirage of a faithful and loving girl friend was often stronger than the

45

truth. Nell's temper, her silences, her pushings away, in fact the real Nell, meant very little because he had convinced himself he was loved. When Nell blew hot rather than cold Luke asked for permission to marry, but this was one instance where hospital staff were strongly against the match, perfectly certain it would never work.

Finally Nell took matters into her own hands: 'I want to go from here, doctor. I'm not happy.'

'What about Luke, Nell?' She shrugged her shoulders.
'There's a small hospital in your home county, Nell.
Would you like me to try and get you there?'
'Have I been there before, doctor?'
'No, you haven't.'
'Right, then, I'll go.'

What state did this leave Luke in? He accepted her departure calmly, for nothing touches him very deeply. He was quickly on the lookout for a new person to call his girl friend.

In one sense, Luke could be said to have made a successful recovery. In the past he needed to expose himself to gain sexual satisfaction, but since his interest in the opposite sex grew he has stopped this behaviour. His schizophrenic relapses are minor and infrequent and he works well. But in an all-important regard, he has not been successful. His emotions are shallow and he feels nothing deeply. Some might say this was due to his mental handicap, but like Nell his early years provided very little opportunity to develop bonds of affection. Both are damaged humans and one wonders if either will ever learn to love deeply.

Ellen

The last illustration is a simple one. It is written because there are some who still cannot conceive of a mongol having normal physical wants. Ellen is 30 and promiscuous. She lives in a mental-handicap hospital which has married quarters and an operational policy which allows for friendship, engagement, pre-marital counselling, and marriage. Couples can proceed to married quarters and hopefully are discharged to supervised bed-sitting rooms on a local guardianship scheme with work each day at the hospital sheltered workshop. Talk is free and basic among married couples and others alike, and the hospital sheltered community encourages its residents to freely shop and circulate in local villages. They are taught to navigate streets and shops safely and satisfactorily. Ellen usually goes with a female partner in the same ward. After one of these expeditions some years ago, Ellen and her friend returned somewhat untidy and reported that they had had a new game with two of the local village youths. As far as we can judge the boys had twirled them round, then hugged and kissed them with gusto. Ellen explained that it was a rather more violent game than she was used to, and she was rather breathless, but she said she liked it, she was not upset and she looked forward to repeating the event.

Ever since, Ellen has thoroughly enjoyed this new dimension. She explained that she never thought she would take to what she calls 'this kissing game', but being a friendly, cheery, happy soul, she now teaches it to any of the boys who takes her fancy. Some of these are backward, some are shy – Ellen's extrovert behaviour often surprises them into taking a new interest in life. She has been counselled that while holding hands and kissing is all right, teasing boys has real dangers, and sexual intercourse is unwise. She pursues her cheery way.

People came and went quite unpredictably in Barry's world and there was no real chance to develop any strong bond with staff or fellow resident. Probably he never will do so. This is not because he was born with 47 chromosomes, but because of the circumstances in which he grew up. Betty loves Paul greatly and like many another wife, sticks to her man through thick and thin. An outsider might think she deserves better, but she herself feels fulfilled in a way she never did when she was on her own. Linda has discovered new maturity in her concern that she and Tom should share their future as man and wife. Bill and Ida ask for no more in life than that they should be together. They do not doubt they will always love each other, and neither does anyone else who knows them. Luke's new girl friend may be more equable in temper than Nell, but it is likely she will want more from him than he is now capable of giving. And what of Nell? For her the grass will always be greener on the far side of the fence. Her mood swings and distrust of people make her a prickly and unlovely character. Her relationship with Luke never really touched her basic experience that everyone, sooner or later, lets you down. Ellen enjoys flirting enormously, giving and getting a great deal of pleasure from her activities. She hurts no one, for she makes it quite clear she will soon be moving on. Like many another flirt, she may one day fall in love and wish to settle down.

We have tried to show that the range of emotion and feelings generated by interpersonal relationships varies greatly. That variety is not due to the degree of mental handicap, but to the different life experiences each partner brings to the interaction. Giving and receiving love, including physical satisfaction, is not the prerogative of those above a certain IQ level; being incapable of anything more than a superficial relationship is not an inherent feature of mental handicap. Love can raise some from apathy, others from despair or loneliness and give meaning to life to many who have lost it. We also feel it can decrease retardation.

6 Marriage and the mentally handicapped

'I have a right to live my happiness, don't I?'
A severely subnormal young woman, hand in hand
with her fiancé

How do the mentally handicapped fare in marriage? How do they cope with such a close and intimate relationship? How much support do they require? So far there has only been one major study in Britain of mentally handicapped married couples – that carried out by Janet Mattinson, and published in 1970.[1] Her findings are instructive. She looked at 32 married couples (out of a list of 40, 4 were untraceable and 4 had separated) who had in their single days all been labelled subnormal (Stanford-Binet IQ range 38–93) and institutionalized in the Royal Western Counties Hospital. She examined whether they were capable of maintaining a living in the community – caring for a home, bringing up children, securing an employment position – and how much support they required in day-to-day living.

About one-third were well housed and had been for a number of years (with very few rent arrears). A third were in less stable accommodation; the remaining third were movers and shifters. The number of children was small (42, of whom 2 had died) – an average of 1.5, which is lower than the national average for the same age group. Many couples were using contraceptives. Of these 40 children 6 (from three families) had been removed from parental care. Only 3 of the 40 were retarded in their development. Twelve husbands had been in regular employment for a number of years; 14 were in less regular employment; only 6 were permanently out of a job. A quarter of the couples were not known to any social worker, or even to the mental welfare officer; another quarter were receiving intensive help.

Miss Mattinson rated marital relationships according to subjective criteria, i.e. whether the partners themselves thought the marriage satisfactory and satisfying. Nineteen couples felt their partnership to be supportive and affectionate; 6 couples did not resent their union and were basically caring and affectionate, but there were symptoms of stress. There were 4 partnerships where one partner depended heavily on the other and both partners expressed resentment about this sort of relationship. Three couples acknowledged their partnership was unsatisfactory but showed evidence of a strong negative tie. One of the conclusions Miss Mattinson reached was (*op. cit.*, p. 201): 'Singly, [the couples] once showed themselves to be defective in social living; paired, with renewed motivation to succeed, and more often than not reinforcing each other's strengths, many of them established marriages which were by no means defective.'

Survey of mentally handicapped married couples in Wales

In 1974 we carried out a survey of marriages where one or both partners had been labelled as mentally defective or subnormal by a consultant in subnormality in Wales. When we analysed this group we found some over IQ 68 (Wechsler IQ 68, i.e. 2 standard deviations below average, is the commonly regarded cut-off point between the dull-normal and the subnormal) who would now be labelled personality disordered (PD), some over IQ 68 once educationally subnormal (ESN), some subnormal under IQ 68 (SN) and some severely subnormal under IQ 50 (SSN).

We originally located 25 such partnerships, using contacts with hospital and social services throughout Wales. The marriages varied in duration from 1 month to 25 years. One partnership had broken up after 2½ years.

It is important to be clear about the degree of handicap in each marriage, for it might be assumed that those handicapped people with 'normal' partners fare better than those with equal or more severe handicap.

Table 6.1   *Degree of handicap in the 25 marriages*

Husbands	N	PD/md	Wives ESN	SN	SSN	MI
5 N			1	3	1	
5 PD/md	3			2		
4 ESN	1			3		
8 SN	1			5	2	
1 SSN					1	
2 MI				2		
	5	0	1	15	4	0

Key
N	Normal
PD/md	Personality disordered/moral defective
ESN	Educationally subnormal
SN	Subnormal
SSN	Severely subnormal
MI	Mentally ill

In fact our findings agreed with other studies – that there was little or no correlation between degree of handicap and success of the partnership either in subjective or objective terms.

As might be expected, the support being received varied. Some had *total support*, i.e. they were within a hospital setting where staff were readily available, where no rent was charged for accommodation, and main meals were provided. Some were in *hostel care*, sometimes responsible for their own domestic arrangements, paying something towards their keep and travelling independently to their place of work. In this category we have also included a couple living in a bungalow complex grouped around an old people's home, visited daily by a staff member. Others were *independent with support* – they lived in the community but received help from relatives/friends/social workers on a fairly regular basis. Lastly, there were those who were *independent without support*, couples now unknown to social services or no longer visited, coping in much the same way as their neighbours.

Table 6.2   *Support being received – intact marriages*

| Degree of Support | Most handicapped partner | | | | |
	PD	ESN	SN	SSN	Total
Total support			2		2
Hostel care			2	1	3
Independent with support		1	10	3	14
Independent without support	3	1	1		5

Support being received is not, of course, the same as 'support needed', although there did seem to be a reasonable fit between the two. There were a few discrepancies – the 2 couples getting 'total support' did not require such a degree of help. Other chance factors were involved, particularly the shortage of accommodation in a resort area. Three of the 'independent with support' couples had a tacit arrangement with Social Services. As one of them said: 'We know where the office is. We go if we want anything.' This may have meant an under-usage of the support available.

There was no correlation between the degree of handicap and type of accommodation the couples were in. None of the 4 partnerships with an SSN member needed hospital accommodation. As many as 20 couples lived in the community, most in self-contained flats or houses. Two more lived in local-authority hostels. As with the general population, housing is often a matter of chance circumstances – of the 2 couples in hospital married-quarters, one had returned from a bedsitting-room after a disagreement with the landlady, the other had recently married and were expected to be able to cope quite adequately in the community once a flatlet had been found.

Table 6.3 *Marital rating – all marriages*

Marital rating	Most handicapped partner:				
	PD	ESN	SN	SSN	Total
Mutually supportive	1	1	8	1	11
Affectionate but symptoms of stress			1	1	2
One partner heavily dependent on other, some resentment			3	2	5
Acknowledged unsatisfactory, but strong negative tie			2		2
Divorced/separated			1		1
Not known	2	1	1		4

For a rating of the marital relationships we have followed Janet Mattinson.[2]

There were few children among those where the wives were of child-bearing age. In most instances this was due to various birth-control methods. There were 14 children in 6 families, all being cared for by their parents. Those of school age were all attending normal infant or junior schools. It is probable that the families are not yet complete, and the sample is too small as yet for any conclusion to be drawn, but only one, then 10 months old, was thought by a health visitor to be marginally backward.[3]

To say each marriage is unique is, of course, a truism, but it does warn us that we can so easily lose sight of individuals in talking about '25 mentally handicapped married couples'. Facts and figures are only half the story, and cannot capture the rich variety of their life styles.

Our most handicapped pair

Being severely subnormal might be thought to be an unsurmountable barrier to marriage, to coping with such a close relationship. After all, many normal people fail. But the severely subnormal can give to and get from each other much comfort and satisfaction.

Bill and Ida (SSN/SSN)
Both partners were originally classified as severely subnormal. They have been in care for much of their lives.

Bill is now 48. He had been living in hospitals, a hostel and lodgings for twenty years and was incapable of looking after himself as his personal hygiene left much to be desired (he dribbled from his urinary system, through laziness rather than physical defect). He was slovenly in his dress and hangdog in expression.

His wife, Ida is 43. She is small and thin, with a pronounced squint in one eye. She was the illegitimate child of a certified mental defective and has spent all her life in care. They met in one hospital many years ago and liked each other, but Ida was moved somewhere else and Bill 'broke his heart'.

By chance the system reunited them some fifteen years later when both attended the same day hospital. They were engaged for two years, Bill had a vasectomy, and they were married in 1972. They have a flatlet in a village close to Bryn y Neuadd and travel in daily by public transport to the sheltered workshops. Ida does her best to keep Bill up to the mark in his dress and he has mastered his dribble. There is a spring in his step, he looks up rather than down, his shoulders are erect; he is a man, and here is his woman to prove it.

They receive support from the hospital social worker and the community domiciliary nursing staff. Of course they also support each other in many ways – and are aware of it. When asked how often they quarrelled, Ida said: 'We do sometimes, but we're friends after.' Bill added: 'I never would hit her, I owe her too much.'

Their relationship is very close. They have few friends but find abiding pleasure in each other's company. The sexual side of their marriage gives them great satisfaction. In answer to the question, they looked at each other and smiled, Bill took Ida's hand and said: 'It ought to be all right, we've been married so long.' They can often be seen walking hand in hand along the seafront, happily engrossed in one another.

Negative ties

The path of many marriages, handicapped or otherwise, is not smooth. Most of us have asked ourselves at one time or another, 'Why on earth do X and Y stick together? I'd never put up with that behaviour.' It may be habit, it may be fear, or ignorance of alternatives; it may also be because of something an outsider cannot see – a joint need is being met.

Dick and Joan (MI/SN)

> O, don't the days seem lank and long
> When all goes right and nothing goes wrong,
> And isn't your life extremely flat
> With nothing whatever to grumble at!
>
> W.S. Gilbert, *Princess Ida*

The longest married couple in our survey, married for 25 years, were judged to have a *strong but negative tie*. Their married life has been full of upset and incident, with heavy involvement of all social services.

Dick has a history of schizophrenia which recurs periodically; but as the social worker says: 'Little wonder – living with Joan would drive an angel mad.' Dick is now 54, a withdrawn, well-built man with a thatch of grey hair.

Joan is subnormal, a cheeky, tubby little barrel of a woman, hardly ever silent, chivvying and scrounging from all and sundry, but with more than a trace of charm. Soon after their marriage Joan was arrested for stealing an overcoat for Dick and they were separated for seven years as Joan was transferred from prison to a subnormality hospital. Visiting time became a nightmare for the staff as Dick and Joan made valiant efforts to make up for lost opportunities and were not inhibited even by being placed in the centre of the corridor.

Joan's incorrigible interest in everyone's business, their

habit of scrounging and foraging and their general life style with rumbustious ups and downs, have taxed community tolerance greatly. In fact the social worker has been hard put to keep a roof over their heads; they have moved almost a score of times. The local housing authority has been reluctant to be of assistance since Dick's accident with an oil stove, while Joan was ill in hospital, which resulted in the beautiful new council maisonette going up in flames.

Suspicion and distrust by each partner of the other's sexual behaviour has been a fundamental cause of friction. Joan came to believe that Dick's one purpose in life was to deceive her with other women. Her fear became so acute that she used to padlock him in the cottage each time she went to the outside toilet. She complained to the social worker that Dick was over-sexed and would not leave her alone. Because of her distraught state the social worker got pills prescribed for the luckless Dick, but within a short space of time Joan was back saying Dick did not want her any more, he must be getting satisfaction elsewhere. The poor social worker did not know where he was.

But now sex has been relegated to the background, they sleep apart and have not had intercourse for several years. They are not lost for other things to disagree over. Asked how often they have arguments Joan said cheerfully, 'Oh, every day. There's some'at all the while.' Had the police ever had to come and see them? 'Good God, yes. Very often,' said Joan. 'There'd be a row between us and we'd be fighting. He's knocked me down more than once.' Had they thought of separating? 'No, we had to put up with it.' Indeed they may drive each other to distraction, but the tie between them is very strong. When Dick was admitted to mental hospital during a schizophrenic episode Joan hitched the forty odd miles down to see him twice a week, regular as clockwork.

Joan is not without insight and summed up the situation rather nicely: 'I heard them say I was a mental defective, whatever that is, but I'm not crazy. I know I'm a bit childish, but someone's got to be better than Dick.' And as Dick said simply: 'Her sees to me.'

The taming of the shrew

Many a parent has watched in amazement as their seemingly completely self-centred son or daughter has married and revealed hidden strengths and talents. Marriage can settle people down and change them remarkably.

Jim and Sarah (SN/SN)

> For I will board her though she chide as loud
> As thunder, when the clouds in autumn crack.
>
> *The Taming of the Shrew*

Sarah, as Jim succinctly put it, 'was a bugger at times'. She had a violent temper and threw tantrums whenever thwarted. Jim, a perky little man, the size of a jockey, is an unlikely looking Petruchio, but showed his mettle from their first encounter.

They were both lodged in the same boarding-house. Sarah, in a rage, had locked her bedroom door and, from her sanctuary, was engaged in a slanging match with the landlady. Jim entered the scene, slightly drunk from his lunchtime pub visit, and took over from the distraught lady of the house. He hammered so violently on the door that it flew open and he then proceeded to give the startled Sarah a piece of his mind. The courtship had started. The proposal was equally stormy. They quarrelled while walking along the promenade and Jim in exasperation said: 'I'll bloody marry you before I've finished.' And he did.

Jim and Sarah have been married now for six years and the change in Sarah is remarkable. She has an air of calmness and contentment, previously absent; she talks quietly and sensibly. They live in very seedy conditions – a flatlet with paint peeling from the walls and the ceiling stained with evidence of upstairs overflows. The double bed with its grey sheets and grubby coverlet is also used as the work surface for sawing logs for the winter fire.

But these two are happy and contributing members of society. Jim has been a full-time maintenance man at a local holiday camp for six years and Sarah works there each summer. In fact it is a sort of 'his and hers' job – he is responsible for the male toilets, Sarah cleans the female ones. They receive minimal support, being unvisited by a social worker, but calling occasionally at the social services department if a need arises. In general their philosophy is simple: 'If we're short we do without. We don't ask from nobody.'

As might be expected, their sexual relationship is completely satisfactory. 'Oh, no problem', said Jim. Sarah has a cap to prevent pregnancy. They do not want children. 'It's best not to have the worry.'

Marriage has certainly worked for them, providing companionship and satisfaction. Sarah said thoughtfully: 'I wouldn't like to be on my own again.' Jim went a stage further: 'Everyone should get married and be happy.'

Stooping to conquer

People choose their marriage partners to meet a number of their needs. A woman may be happiest where she can 'mother' her husband; a man may feel more secure with an older woman, or need to 'stoop to conquer' to sustain erections. As long as there is little or no discrepancy between the roles one partner assigns to the other and elects to play himself, the partnership is usually successful.

Derek and Pam (PD/SN)

Derek is 29, a sharp-tongued man with a permanent air of 'They can't pull the wool over my eyes!' His IQ is within the dull–normal range, but he was placed in the subnormality system on a Section 65 Order after a long history of indecent assaults on children. By chance he discovered his own solution to his behavioural problems. In hospital he met a girl who thought he was wonderful and who told him so. This was a heady, new experience for Derek, and one which opened up new possibilities for him. With a social age of 7 or 8, Pam was quite content for Derek to take the lead, and he did so with increasing self-confidence. 'I can make something of this girl. I'll show everyone she's not stupid,' he said.

They married three years ago with the approval of Derek's parents, but unbeknown to the hospital

authorities; and apart from one probably innocent
incident he has kept clear of children. Instead he has Pam,
a wife who idolizes him, with whom he can and does
adopt a paternal role. 'He doesn't like me to call him
Derek,' she said. 'I call him Pop.' His social worker says
Derek seems to gain strength from Pam's dependence on
him; his parents, with whom they live, feel that the
marriage has settled Derek's social and sexual
misbehaviour.

And what of Pam, usually keeping quiet in the
background? True, she is probably under-functioning
because it suits everyone in the household to have it so,
but she, too, has gained something. She has improved her
social and domestic skills under her mother-in-law's
guidance, Derek cares a great deal for her and they have
many outings together. 'I want to teach her as much as I
can,' he says, 'so that when I'm not here, die like, she
won't have to go back into hospital.' Pam is by no means
unhappy or discontented with her lot.

Perhaps the real test will come when the couple achieve
the ambition of a council house or flat of their own. Yet
the marriage does have strength and at the moment is
answering the needs of both partners.

Pressures of opinion

Children can and often do cement the marriage bond, but
we know from statistics that entering marriage because of
pregnancy can be a cause of stress in the subsequent partnership. Where one or both partners are additionally handicapped the strain of adjusting to each other and of being
new parents may be very great indeed.

Freddie and Alice (ESN/SN)
In other circumstances Freddie and Alice would probably
not have married, but Alice became pregnant and
refused the recommended abortion. Freddie's brother
said: 'Why don't you two get married?' It hadn't
occurred to them, but it seemed like a good idea.

Freddie is 29, a tough-looking, self-confident young

man, son of a subnormal mother, categorizing himself as ESN. He was placed in a subnormality hospital after disturbances in the community and the alleged assault of a policeman. There he met Alice, a small, haggard subnormal woman who seems older than her 38 years. She had been raised by her grandmother after her father had been jailed for the manslaughter of her mother, and entered a children's home at 14 after committing larceny, the old lady having died and father's care being judged unsatisfactory.

They were married a year ago, three months before the birth of their twins, and moved into hostel accommodation. Although they receive much assistance with housework and care of the twins, Alice has been finding it difficult to cope. As she says: 'I pick one up, and the other one's crying.' Freddie, urged by Alice to stay home and help her, lost his job because of bad time-keeping. Being cooped up together with the babies leads to short tempers, and hostel staff have had some fears for the children. They do not go out together in the evenings – Freddie disappears down to the pub to meet his mates, leaving Alice behind. She gets depressed and moody, and has walked out on him twice. They quarrel frequently, usually over the babies' care. The more competent Freddie gets impatient with Alice's dependence on him for assistance. To his credit though, he arranged quite on his own initiative to have a vasectomy when he found Alice was afraid to have a sterilization operation. Both are relieved there will be no more children. Freddie talks of getting a council house in his home town, and wants to move from the hostel, a place where he feels he does not belong, but realizes Alice would have great difficulty in managing the twins alone.

Neither feel marriage has changed them at all. Alice has not yet come to terms with her new situation, resenting, yet depending on, help from Freddie and staff. Freddie, while in the main supportive and proud of his children, continues to act as if he was single as far as evening entertainment goes. The stresses are great at the moment, but as the children grow the circumstances will obviously change.

Many of the problems that the couples encountered might have arisen in any marriage; mother-in-law interference, sexual disharmony, housing difficulties. The difference, of course, often lies in their ability to cope. This is where support can be so vital. Dick and Joan have needed assistance in major areas – housing, employment, health – but not all couples require such an input. Many of the spouses have long histories of hospitalization and lack firsthand experience of family life. This can sometimes turn molehills into mountains. Betty (SN), orphaned at an early age, had lived in homes and institutions nearly all her life until marriage. Always a neat and tidy woman, she complained in tears to the social worker that however much she appealed to him, her husband Paul (PD) refused to hang up his clothes and they lay as they fell around the bedroom. A woman-to-woman chat about the shortcomings of husbands in general, introducing the idea that other wives also get upset sometimes by their partner's habits, reduced the mountain to size, and a talk to Paul prompted him to be a bit more thoughtful.

We are certainly not equating marriage with complete independence; indeed, most 'normal' marriages receive moral, practical and financial support at some point, especially in their early stages. The amount of help needed to maintain the mentally handicapped couples will differ both in intensity and time span, but this would be so for the partners, married or single. It seems just as sensible to care for people in units of two, as it does for individuals, for while the nature of their problems may change with marriage, we have not found that they increase significantly.

In the last analysis, marriage is a contract which primarily has to satisfy the partners themselves. How did they feel about their change of status?

'I'm happier than I was. I had no one before.'
'We're completely together, no one can separate us. It's just great, you know.'
'I do think he's a good husband, more than I can tell you.'
'I thought I'd never get married. I don't regret it one bit.'
'He's a good lad, he looks after me.'

'She's good to me, a good wife. I wouldn't part with her even if someone give me a thousand pounds.'

In fact most of those interviewed said they were happier and more settled now they were married. Companionship overcame loneliness and was a source of great comfort. In this major respect, marriages between those we call 'mentally handicapped' and those we call 'normal' differ not at all.

7

The law

How far does the law allow care staff to help the handicapped? If words, pictures and films do not add up to practicality, as our married handicapped couples tell us, are care staff allowed to go further? A parent may be legally entitled to teach his child to masturbate to relieve tension. Is this permissible for care staff? Should one leave morals or ethics aside here, or as the Swedes suggest in this very private area, should we *not* talk too much about it since individuals vary so much in their feelings to each other, both positive and negative? Yet what if parent or staff is 'caught'? It is a very grey area for most people. What follows is an account of a discussion between a psychiatrist and a barrister interested in the field, but cannot be regarded as 'counsel's opinion'. In a field as yet virtually untried by case law, each employing authority is entitled to its own view, which means that the first case will be tried on its own particular merits.

The law in relation to sex for the handicapped in England and Wales has not changed greatly in recent years, in spite of our so-called permissive society. The 1959 Mental Health Act did away with the old Board of Control strictures on the sex life of the mentally handicapped and only one of its definitions, that of the severely subnormal, was carried back to the 1956 Sexual Offences Act which technically renders it an offence to have sexual intercourse with one who is severely subnormal.

In practice any prosecutions under these Acts have been rare, and commonly failed. This is because the definition of a severely subnormal person is rather a narrow one, and in practice, although the onus of proof is on the defendant, it is a valid defence for the accused without specialized knowledge to say that he did not know his partner was severely subnormal, and had no means of knowing. For instance, in a recent prosecution where a man seduced a lady with Down's syndrome (mongolism) in a cupboard in a well-lit cinema, he was able to defend himself by saying that he did not know that his partner was severely subnormal, which indeed she was. The court held that ordinary persons could not be expected to recognize severe subnormality. Thus all normal-looking ambulant persons would be outside this law, because in the absence of anything to the contrary, their 'normal' partner would expect them to be a consenting citizen.

Sex has also become relatively common in mental-handicap hospitals, as their residents move freely about the community as part of the 'normalization' programme. So far as we are aware, no prosecutions have been known to succeed as the result of this. Of course, most partners chosen by hospital residents are usually hospital residents themselves, and it is perfectly obvious that such persons would not be proceeded against by the police.

Marriage among mentally handicapped is also becoming common. The procedure here is for the hospital's Responsible Medical Officer to state on the case notes that in his medical opinion the resident concerned understands the nature of what he or she is proposing to undertake, whereupon the said person is then entitled to sign (or mark with a cross) and thus validate the marriage certificate. So, in law, a citizen with Down's syndrome (mongolism) is perfectly legally entitled to get married although it would be wise for such a person to have a medical certificate in his or her possession at the time, in case the Registrar of Marriages should ask for it. This would also protect the married subnormal member against any action for annulment at a later date by the other partner should he or she change their mind.

Homosexual partnerships are still proscribed under English law when one of the partners is under 21 and particularly so if one is under 16. This is still an area where numerous prosecutions take place. If a mentally handicapped man wishes to live in sexual partnership with another person of like homosexual inclination, he must make sure that that partner is above the age of 21, and not severely subnormal. Under Section 1 of the Sexual Offences Act 1956 a severely subnormal man cannot validly give the consent which would make a homosexual act in private between males lawful. The consent of the Director of Public Prosecutions is required before a case can be brought, and where one of the parties is under 16 this will almost certainly be given.

A successful prosecution would be difficult if there was no corroborative evidence. Corroboration has been defined as independent evidence, confirming other evidence, which not only shows the crime was committed, but that the accused committed it. It does not necessarily have to be the evidence of a witness – in some cases it can be circumstantial, or that of a scientific expert. Willing partners in a homosexual act are regarded as accomplices, and a judge is required to warn the jury of the dangers of convicting on an accomplice's evidence without corroboration. If an adult witness is unfit to take the oath, the statutes do not demand corroboration as a matter of law, but if the judge failed to direct the jury accordingly, it seems unlikely a conviction could stand. There is another aspect here which bears mention. Since 1967, homosexual acts in private between consenting adults have been legal. But just where in a hospital or hostel is a private place if one's bed is in a shared room or dormitory and the toilets are communal? Are the mentally handicapped in care deprived of the rights enjoyed by citizens outside because there is no privacy?

Anal sex between male and female was always a common-law offence. It remains illegal according to the Sexual Offences Act 1956. There is no proviso in the Act for a circumstance where disability prevents vaginal intercourse, and there is no exemption for consenting husband and wife. Since the parties will be accomplices as defined in Baskerville,[1] the jury is entitled to seek corroboration and today it seems unlikely that any jury would ever convict. The position is especially incongruous in view of the relaxation of the law in favour of consenting adult males for such acts in private.

There is no legal proscription against oral sex between males, or males and females over 16, but below this age there is a possibility of prosecution for indecent assault under the Sexual Offences Act 1956, generally against the male, since consent cannot validly be given by a girl under 16. Similarly consent cannot be given at any age by someone who is severely subnormal, but it is a valid defence for the accused to show he did not know, and had no reason to suspect, the accused was severely subnormal, as has been previously explained. The defence that an act of oral sex is not an assault but an endearment is probably not available. Today, however, it seems a jury will be most reluctant to convict. This is due to a change of attitude, not law, and the inherent right of the jury to return what the lawyers would term a 'perverse' verdict. Perhaps one should regard this as 'law reform by jury'.

A problem may arise when mentally handicapped persons commit any sexual act in public, such as indecent exposure. At common law it is held that no intention to cause disgust or annoyance is required for a conviction for indecency in public. There are, of course, regular prosecutions of teenagers for such activities on the beach every summer, generally resulting in a small fine.

The employment of surrogates to help overcome specific sexual difficulties is a relatively new field, although the idea of courtesans assisting in the sex education of young men is well known in social history and literature. Surrogates may be defined as persons neutral in affection or charitable in intent, who engage in sexual activities with their clients to improve their mental state. If no money or valuable consideration passes, an essential in the definition of prostitution is lacking. Even if such services were paid for it is hard to see the second part of the definition, i.e. 'common lewdness', being fulfilled where such help was responsibly prescribed and undertaken with a therapeutic motive. Fortunately the House of Lords has recently held that today the courts have no reserve power to create new crimes at common law.

However, if it was found that prostitution was committed, any *man* who took any fee for facilitating this service could be convicted under Section 30(1) of the Sexual Offences Act 1956. Further, since it is equally prostitution for a man to service either a female or another male for money if the act amounts to common lewdness, Section 5 of the Sexual Offences Act 1967 applies where the prostitute is a male. Both men and women can be convicted of living off the prostitution of a man under this Section of the Act.

A clinic where acts amounting to prostitution took place would be a brothel if more than one prostitute operated there. Those managing it could be prosecuted under Section 33 of the Sexual Offences Act, 1956. Under Section 31 of this Act, a woman who for purposes of gain exercises control or influence over a prostitute's movements in a way which shows she is aiding, abetting or compelling the prostitution, commits an offence. The tenant or occupier of the clinic could be prosecuted under Section 36 of the Act if he knowingly permitted the use of the premises for habitual prostitution. Lastly, it could constitute an offence if the organizer asked a *woman* to act as a surrogate should the service be deemed prostitution.

Currently, the only well-known surrogate service in England and Wales is one in Birmingham, and, as those concerned have avoided the pitfalls mentioned, there has been no police intervention. Certainly if all elements of prostitution are avoided and confidentiality is observed, there is no offence known to the law.

All male staff and managers of mental hospitals or mental nursing homes are forbidden by Section 128 of the Mental Health Act 1959 to have unlawful sexual intercourse (i.e. outside marriage) with a *woman* who is being treated for mental disorder. There can be no prosecution without the consent of the Director of Public Prosecutions. The Sexual Offences Act 1967 (Section 1) prohibits acts of buggery or gross indecency between a man on the staff of a hospital or otherwise responsible for mental patients and a male patient.

Sexual relations between a female mental-hospital staff member and a female patient could be construed as ill-treatment. With more difficulty, this could also apply if the staff member was a woman and the patient male. Ill-treatment is a separate criminal offence under Section 126 of the Mental Health Act 1959, but the ordinary laws of assault also apply. If a male subnormal patient over 21 consented to sexual relations with a female member of staff, this would fall more readily into the area of professional ethics than of law. In any particular instance this is clearly an area where legal opinion would have to be sought.

It seems from the way Section 128 is worded that a doctor or a nurse of one mental hospital is free to have sexual relations with a patient in another. However, if that patient is severely subnormal he might reasonably be expected to suspect that that was so, because of his specialized knowledge.

A staff member teaching masturbation, or masturbating a patient who cannot perform this act himself, stands in danger of the law if that patient is under 21, or is over 21 but severely subnormal. If corroborative evidence can be brought the staff member might be charged under the indecency laws.

Staff are expected to perform a number of personal acts for patients in their care (bathing, dressing, toileting) and there is a case for regarding masturbation as an act in this category. However, this is an ethical, not a legal, debate. It may be that a hospital or hostel staff who after due deliberation with the area health authority or social services committee agreed on a policy allowing masturbation of patients by staff under specific conditions, would be on fairly strong legal ground. But, as far as we know, this has not been put to the test. Until it is, staff are vulnerable.

To sum up:

1 The severely subnormal are especially protected by law against sexual exploitation.

2 A severely subnormal patient who wished to marry must have a certificate from the Responsible Medical Officer stating he/she understands the nature of the undertaking. It is not necessary, but might be advisable, for a subnormal patient to have the same in case it is required by the Registrar of Marriages.

3 Homosexual acts are illegal: in public; where one partner is under 21; and where one partner is severely subnormal.

4 Heterosexual anal sex remains illegal, although it is doubtful any jury would convict if both adults were willing partners. Oral sex in private between adults is not illegal.

5 One of the commonest police charges against mentally handicapped persons is that of indecent assault or indecent exposure. No intention to cause disgust or annoyance is required for a prosecution.

6 So far no surrogate attached to a clinic specializing in the treatment of sexual difficulties has been prosecuted for prostitution.

7 Male staff and managers are legally proscribed from having unlawful sexual intercourse with female patients being treated for mental disorder, and from sexual relations with male patients. Female staff are not so proscribed, but such acts would contravene professional ethics, and might occasion charges of ill-treatment. Staff are at risk of a charge of indecent assault if they help patients to masturbate as a person-to-person service. No case law exists where masturbation has been performed as 'treatment', carried out on medical advice, or after case conference, but where new treatment procedures are carried out after 'due care and deliberation' the judge commonly gives the benefit of his doubt to the defendant.

The law acts as a safeguard, protecting the helpless from the unscrupulous, but where it can be shown that the service provided is, in professional judgment, a positive aid to the handicapped, it would be expected to protect those providing such services.

8 Setting up a health and sex-education programme

Obviously no hard and fast rules can be made in planning and implementing such a programme. Some suggested topics are given at the end of this chapter but the list is by no means exhaustive and no doubt readers will think of others.

A few guidelines may serve here to focus attention on the most important considerations involved and answer some of the 'who', 'what', and 'how' question which arise.

1 Liaison with parents/care staff/administrators

Schools as a matter of course inform parents that unless they raise an objection their child will receive a course of health and sex education. A Special School would be advised to hold a meeting (or several) of parents to talk through the very real anxieties they will naturally feel.

Some parents will feel they are the best people to educate their children as far as sex is concerned. This is, of course, their right. They may, however, welcome some advice about what sort of books would be helpful in supplementing their talks. Other parents will feel embarrassed about speaking to their children or adolescents about sex, and feel relieved the whole topic is to be covered by a professional. If there is

70

close family contact, as with day-school attenders, adolescents and adults at training centres, or those going home most weekends, parents will play an important part in backing up what is being taught. To do this they must be clear about the topics covered, so they need to be as closely involved as possible. It is likely many would like a preview of any audio-visual material included in the programme.

Administrators and senior care staff of hostels and hospitals should be kept in the picture as such a programme is planned. It may also be advisable to invite the local newspaper to run a feature on the whole range of social training being given to the mentally handicapped hostel/hospital residents to encourage them to be more independent and less in need of an expensive hostel/hospital place.

2 Parental concerns

Some parents are afraid that their mentally handicapped offspring will not be able to control their sexual impulses, and thus will get themselves into trouble or be a prey to exploitation. On the one hand they fear any expression of sexuality, on the other they worry that tension will build and cause some sort of behavioural explosion. Many ignore or deny the sexuality of their handicapped child. Consequently any obvious manifestation of interest is seen in terms of a 'problem', something to be stopped. They need to be helped to see that like all humans their child has sexual impulses and drives. They need help in setting realistic targets for sexual behaviour, and it should be emphasized that this behaviour is made up of a very wide repertoire. Sexual intercourse is by no means the only way comfort and satisfaction can be achieved. Parents of boys are often anxious about masturbation and how they should deal with it. They need reassurance that it is a normal expression of sexuality and not a harmful or dirty habit. Most mentally handicapped adolescents are quite capable of learning that, like toileting, masturbation is a private behaviour. If it persists as a public display parents should ask themselves whether there is a physical reason, e.g. clothing too tight or a minor irritation, or a social reason, e.g. attention-seeking, or perhaps not sufficient physical activity during the day. It needs to be clearly stated that the mentally handicapped need *more* help not *less* in understanding themselves, their bodies and their feelings. Parents should be clear that the true choice before them is not *whether* to give their children a form of sex education, but *which* form. For, as Kempton[1] points out: sex education begins at birth; attitudes are developed and sensual pleasures are learned from infancy in many and various ways. It goes on all the time and from many different media. Parents should be helped to understand that sex education includes learning about *relationships*, about *physiology*, and about the stimulation and control of *body feelings*. Sex education does *not* give rise to experimentation, nor stimulate sexual activity; rather it acts as a deterrent, for it teaches responsibility and control. Sex education cannot be premature – a child will only learn what he can understand, but it may come too late to prevent unnecessary worry to the mentally handicapped, their parents or care staff.

3 Who teaches?

There is no one 'obvious' choice here – there are many options. The most important consideration is that the person concerned feels confident to talk about personal subjects in a matter-of-fact and basic way and knows both the facts and the residents in the group. A sense of humour and an honest, direct approach are very necessary.

A teacher in a Special School who takes the senior pupils would be the most suitable person to explore 'growing up' and its implications in a regular lesson period. Lower down the school a less formal approach may be more appropriate, making use of 'the teachable moment', dealing with topics as they naturally arise, for example at the birth of a younger brother or sister for one of the class. Health education is covered just as naturally – keeping clean, going to the toilet, what happens inside our bodies, etc.

Many Special Schools watch television programmes such as the BBC *'Merry Go Round'*. This can be a helpful lead-in to a talk or discussion.

In hospitals and hostels, care staff, if not actively involved in the teaching itself, should always be made aware of what topics are being covered. Residents may need to ask their favourite staff member to make clear things they did not follow in the group. Sometimes it is only a small misunderstanding, but it could lead to embarrassment. One young man came back to the ward for his lunch saying he'd had a very interesting lesson, all about peanuts and undercoats. After some puzzling the staff were able to correct his pronunciation. He had misheard two words new to him – 'penis' and 'intercourse'.

A nurse, a further-education teacher, social worker or a psychologist may well be involved in sex education. It is not so much *who*, but *how* and *what* that are important.

4 Constructing the programme

This may well take several months as the group leaders bring their own knowledge up to date, the ground is prepared, and the material reviewed. At the end of this chapter we suggest a list of topics which might be covered. This can, of course, be modified according to local need.

Using audio-visual aids can be most helpful but, in the absence of anything produced specifically for the mentally handicapped, discussion-group leaders should approach the material carefully. Sometimes the commentary is confusing or the slide pictures raise more questions than they answer. For instance, we have had residents wondering why their bodies did not have written labels indicating the position of the vagina, penis, etc.

Flexibility has to be the keynote of the whole programme. It must be flexible in overall length, for, besides frequent recaps and revision, leaders will find that just one slide or picture can prompt enough talk and discussion to fill a session. Obviously too rigorous a timetable would cut short some of these helpful information exchanges. It needs to be flexible, too, in its content. For example, some adolescent girls may only be able to grasp the hygiene aspect of menstruation; others will be capable of understanding more and show a lively interest in the whys and wherefores of their body functioning.

Small discussion groups meeting regularly in an informal

atmosphere (easy chairs, over tea or coffee) work best in a hostel or hospital. In Special Schools the number or setting may be different, but basically the same approach is needed – simple explanations, related to their own experiences of changes in the body, and emotional feelings.

5 Where to start

Parents, teachers and care staff are frequently able to say, with a high degree of accuracy, just how well a particular mentally handicapped adolescent can handle money or dress himself, but it is all too likely that they will not be nearly so accurate in estimating the same adolescent's knowledge of sexual matters.[2] Often these are taboo subjects, and therefore not openly discussed.

We know there is much ignorance, but some are more knowledgeable than others. It is helpful to have some idea of what individual members of the group know or do not know before starting.

A word ought to be said here about the terms to use. We obviously defeat our purpose if we use the 'proper' words without relating them to the 'slang' expressions with which the group is far more likely to be familiar. To begin with it is best to use both, for example 'penis' and 'dick' (the penis probably has more slang names than any other part of the body, so use the one or two best known to the group).

6 Severely mentally handicapped students

Severely mentally handicapped individuals may pose special difficulties for parents, teachers and care staff, particularly in their sexual expression. What guidelines can be offered for those concerned with this group? Most importantly, it must be clearly understood that it is *normal* for all humans to develop secondary sexual characteristics, and to want to show and receive affection by touch, warmth and body contact. The biological clocks of severely mentally handicapped individuals may be set at a slightly different rate from those of their normal peers, but set they are and cannot be stopped. Recognition of this is a vital first stage in coping

74

with the sexual expression that can be so upsetting for parents and carers. It leads us to the stance: puberty and attendant emotional changes are going to occur, what is our response going to be?

As with more able mentally handicapped students, it is helpful to discover what individuals *do* know about gender, reproduction and sexual behaviour. Working with a manual such as Fischer *et al.* 1974 allows parent or teacher not only to gauge levels of understanding, but also to become familiar with the language used by the individual to describe behaviour and body function.[3]

Setting goals is an important exercise because it requires us to make decisions about the degree of complexity of our input. For example, what specifically do we want a severely mentally handicapped girl to understand/do about her menstruation? Considerations would be:

(a) It is a normal occurrence, and happens to all women. This can only be got across by the attitude of the person helping the girl.

(b) The girl knows that each time her period starts she must tell (by word or sign) a carer so that she receives the help she needs in managing menstruation.

(c) Can she be taught to care for herself during the period?[4] A behaviour modification programme might achieve this.

(d) The girl maintains modest behaviour, i.e. changes her sanitary pad in private, or with a helper; she does not show or tell everyone else what is happening.

As Winifred Kempton indicates in her description of the Scarborough Method, the most basic component is emotional security (i.e. having periods is normal) and self-care, together with appropriate social behaviour.[5] Explanations can be widened, rather like ripples, from this most simple 'core' according to individuals' level of understanding. In this particular example of menstruation, the next ripple would be the simple biological explanation of periods, the next ripple would consider the relation of the menses to reproduction. Mildly handicapped students may well be able to go even further and grasp the social implications of fertility.

Answering the 'understand/do' question in relation to menstruation is relatively uncomplicated, because it is a clear-cut event. But the question can also aid us in our approach to other areas. It stops us falling into the trap of being overwhelmed by the teaching task, feeling 'they'll never understand anything'. We might draw an analogy with electricity – probably the majority of the population understands little or nothing about the generation, storing and flowing of this energy scource, but this lack of knowledge does not prevent them from effectively (and for the most part safely) using it in all manner of daily tasks. The 'do' component in this instance outstrips 'understanding', but in practical terms this does not matter significantly. While we would want to do our best to help severely mentally handicapped students to understand as much as possible about their bodies, emotions and life events, the 'do' component is always likely to be more important, for it is behaviour, the acting out of feelings and emotions, in which difficulties manifest themselves. The more unacceptable behaviour is, the more restricted and curtailed are opportunities for entertainment, outings or social interaction. As sympathetic parents/carers/teachers, we may be able to guess with some accuracy the feelings and emotions behind a particular behaviour, but we can do little to alter the innate, internal phenomena. We can, however, do something to channel their expression.

Given that it is normal for all humans to have sexual feelings and gain pleasure from warmth and touch, where and with whom in a specific environment can a particular individual express what he feels sexually? If the answer is nowhere and with no one, that should lead to a reassessment. Could more privacy be given, could a more flexible approach be made to students holding hands, hugging, sitting with an arm round each other (always provided the person being touched does not object!). Although it might be argued that schools are not the place for such behaviour, three points are relevant. Firstly, such behaviour *does* occur in any normal mixed school, mostly out of sight of the eyes of authority. Severely handicapped students are rather more efficiently supervised, perhaps overly so. Secondly, more and more

ESN(S) pupils are remaining in education until 19, spending a greater part of their day in the only place where they are able to see their friends. Thirdly, left to themselves, severely mentally handicapped individuals usually do not want to do more than cuddle, kiss, hug or hold hands with a special friend.

Because of its sexual implications, we often feel uneasy about allowing severely mentally handicapped people to touch at all, and tell them off for stroking, patting or embracing. The multiply handicapped are at a particular disadvantage, because at every point they are at the receiving end of touch, touch that is often intimate but impersonal – dressing, toileting, menstrual care, bathing, feeding. One way of giving touch a place is through games and exercises. Here touch and body contact can be encouraged, helping to firm up muscles, relax tenseness, foster confidence and trust, and allowing the opportunity for increased awareness of 'self' and 'other'. Remedial gymnasts and physiotherapists should be able to suggest such activities. Warren's book, *Drama Games for Mentally Handicapped People* also gives plenty of ideas.[6]

What areas should be included in a structured programme for ESN(S) students? Readers will have their own views. Hamre-Nietupski and Williams report on one programme employed with 20 students aged between 12 and 17 whose IQ range was 35-54.[7]

Five main components were devised:

1 Bodily distinction
2 Self-care skills
3 Family members and relationships
4 Social interactions
5 Social manners

Later a second phase built on the skills acquired in the initial programme. Parents and teachers decided that more sophisticated information was required concerning:

1 Growth distinctions and reproduction
2 Self-care skills
3 Social skills and social manners

The authors report that with very few exceptions the students mastered the objectives in the component areas and were also able to generalize their newly acquired understanding. This successful programme is being revised and extended.

Teaching shoud be by means of short, uncomplicated sentences supplemented by simple visual material, such as pictures, body puzzles, felt cloth figures. Social situations and good manners are best acted out to demonstrate appropriate and inappropriate behaviour. Behaviour modification programmes are necessarily systematic, and can be very successful both in teaching specific self-care skills, and in substituting acceptable public behaviour for acts which are unacceptable, such as open masturbation, or potentially dangerous, such as indiscriminate kissing and hugging. Clear and specific corrections of behaviour are needed. 'Don't do that!' 'That's not very nice, is it?' may have very little meaning to the severely mentally handicapped person, particularly if teacher or care staff, because of embarrassment, is half pretending the behaviour is not occurring anyway. The nettle should be more firmly grasped: 'Susan, don't pick your nose.' 'Johnny, don't play with your penis here.' At each correction the words should be accompanied by full, but disapproving attention.

A special word needs to be added concerning inappropriate masturbation. It is this behaviour perhaps more than any other which causes distress to parents and care staff. A number of points need to be made:

1 Masturbation is a natural and normal human activity for both males and females. It is not realistic or desirable to attempt to stop an individual from any and every auto-erotic act.

2 The peak of sexual interest and activity is usually the late teens and early twenties so, in the long term, time will decrease the inclination.

3 Open masturbation may be engaged in for a wide variety of reasons besides the physical release and satisfaction that orgasm brings. It is, for example, an extremely effective means of catching parental or staff attention; also of comforting oneself if something has not gone right. Before

beginning any systematic re-shaping of behaviour, parents/ care staff should keep a record of what was happening immediately before an individual began to masturbate, how long the activity continued, and what happened afterwards. A pattern may emerge, for example it may become obvious that the individual is being excluded from some game or enjoyable pastime, or that a particular person is exciting him. An American manual is available to suggest procedures.[8]

4 Masturbation is a learned behaviour. Most individuals learn by themselves, or with others, the 'trick' of rate, friction and time span needed to bring them to orgasm. But some do not, frequently touching and rubbing, but never continuing long enough to achieve relief. What course should parents or care staff pursue? Many parents report an improvement in behaviour when they have taught their son or daughter how to masturbate successfully. Where the severely mentally handicapped client is in residential care, the approach cannot be made with the same informality or privacy. See Chapter 7 for a comment on the legal position.

If and when the set goals are achieved, continue to reinforce the knowledge and behaviour, and re-consider the position. Have you perhaps underestimated capabilities? Might targets be extended? Begin with the basics and go on as far as you can.

To sum up – what does your severely mentally handicapped child/student need to understand/do for his own protection and to avoid social embarrassment? Set clear, realistic goals. What teaching method, or combination of approaches, can be utilized to achieve these targets? Be as simple and direct as possible.

7 Suggested topics

A health and sex-education programme is best placed in the total context of social training. Biological and physical facts can be used as the starting point for much of the social learning that will help the mentally handicapped understand themselves, and other people, better. For other curriculum suggestions see Craft *et al.*[9]

Biological aspect
How the body works - the skeleton, muscles, skin, heart, the five senses, etc.

Social context
* What is good health? How can we help our bodies work best?
* Personal hygiene.
* Good grooming.
* Safety of self and others in the home and outside. Cause of accidents, danger areas, emergencies.
* Everyone has handicaps of one sort or another. How can they be minimized?

Biological aspect
Puberty - physical changes in adolescents, emotional changes, increase of sexual drive and interest, start of menstruation, nocturnal emissions.

Social context
* How does growing up change us?
* Understanding ourselves and others - recognising our own moods; how we signal what we are feeling (a good introduction here are newspaper and magazine photos of people registering various emotions).
* Daydreams about sex - these are normal and natural, everyone has them. It is *actions* which may get us into trouble.
* Menstrual hygiene and care for girls. Knowledge of menstruation for boys in that they should know why girls are sometimes more 'touchy' or less ready to join in activities.
* Wet dreams - a boy will want reassurance that this is a normal occurrence, one of the signs that he is becoming a young man. Here one could also deal with erections, which sometimes surprise and embarrass a boy.
* Masturbation - this is a normal sexual expression in both males and females, adolescents and adults. From a medical point of view it is not possible to masturbate 'too much', for each body sets its own physical limits. It

is essentially a private activity, as is every sexual act involving the genitals. Most mentally handicapped people can understand this.

* Expressing ourselves and letting others have their say too. Exercising tolerance.
* Relationships with others of the same/opposite sex. Friends and acquaintances - do we behave in the same way to everyone? How do we decide how to behave? How do we try to make friends? What do we look for in a friend?
* Different kinds of love - we use the word in many ways, e.g. a parent for a child, a child for an aunt or uncle, a person for an object (toy, car, steak-and-kidney pie), man for a woman, friend for a friend. Can we 'run out of love' like we do money? Being in love, expressions of love.
* Girl friends/boy friends - what do you expect from them? What do they expect of you?
* Behaviour on a date. How far should petting go?
* Public and private behaviour - is it sometimes different? Why? The group will no doubt be able to list some appropriate and non-appropriate behaviour.
* Good and bad manners.

Biological aspect
Physical differences between adult men and women. Different physical types within one country, different nationalities.

Social context
* Male and female roles - expectations of behaviour.
* Partnership and marriage - What do we look for in a partner? What are the responsibilities of marriage? The advantages and disadvantages?
* Individuality - we are all different, respect for other people's differences, personal worth and esteem.
* Difference between people and objects - people have feelings and can be hurt and upset, or happy and contented. Things cannot be unhappy or glad. Treating

others as we would like to be treated, not 'using' people in a selfish way.

Biological aspect
Male and female reproductive systems – sexual intercourse, conception, pregnancy, birth, needs of babies, young children.

Social context
* Every time a physically mature male and female have sexual intercourse there is a risk of pregnancy. Do we always want to start a baby when we have sex?
* Birth-control techniques, correcting old wives' tales.
* Whose responsibility is it to make sure that a baby is not conceived?
* The responsibilities of parenthood.

Biological aspect
Venereal diseases – causes, sources of infection. Symptoms of each. Harmful effects.

Social context
* Prevention.
* Responsibility to your partner.
* Check-ups and treatment.

The discussions can be as wide-ranging as you and the group want to go. For example, when considering good health, you might talk about use of leisure time. Is it better to spend a Saturday afternoon watching sport on TV or playing football yourself? Growing up and becoming an adult brings responsibilities and you can explore the rights and duties of citizenship. Social training has very many sides to it, but the overall purpose is clear: to aid the mentally handicapped to increase the skills, knowledge and understanding which will help them enrich their lives.

Conclusion

a personal view

It seems only right to end a book of this kind with a personal statement of our conclusions so far and our philosophical approach.

All those who are involved in the care of the handicapped are anxious to aid them in a solution of their own personal difficulties as well as to improve their social abilities. It is common knowledge that many normal adults, quite apart from those who are handicapped, have difficulties in relating to the opposite sex, which can cause great personal unhappiness, they have sexual tensions which occasionally lead them into violence, and may be lonely, leading to depression, perhaps even suicide. Of course, the handicapped share in the needs and strivings of fellow humans. We therefore believe that counselling programmes and living conditions should be evolved to aid them enrich their lives.

Counselling services at their simplest mean that adults who are in contact with the handicapped should have thought out their own answers to sexual needs for themselves and the handicapped with whom they are in contact. Their counselling or talking through should not consist of negative directions such as 'Don't do that', 'That's bad', and the like. Parents, care staff and professionals should be ready with a positive approach so that when they see signs of sexual need or are asked questions of a sexual nature they can say 'That's important' and either discuss the need, there and then, in simple and direct language, or if it is not convenient make a mental note to do so at a later time when it is. Parents, who are naturally in a more direct position for counselling than others, are the most concerned. We hope this book will aid them in thinking about the needs of their adolescent, and provide information about various written and visual material which can be of use. Care staff are often worried about their legal position, which we hope will be clarified by some of the chapters in this book, and for whom we advise that they request the advice of the senior professionals in their field. Nurses in hospitals will expect that the line of approach will be laid down by the legally responsible medical officer, the consultant in charge of the ward in co-operation with his senior nursing advisers. Care staff in local-authority homes would expect to have the policy of that home laid down by the area officer, no doubt after consultation with his director, and the social services committee. We cannot continue to ignore this vital area of human behaviour. Last year the National Development Group for the Mentally Handicapped published a check-list of standards to be used as a measure of the quality of care provided by any service. Sexuality was not neglected. Standard 89 asks 'In order to maximize the client's development and independence, in what ways do staff encourage and train the client (according to the client's individual needs) in social skills . . .' Then follows a whole list of items, one of which is 'Relationships with the Opposite Sex?' The check-list goes on:

> How are staff counselled on how to handle matters concerning the sexual needs and behaviour of clients?

> What arrangements are made for providing counselling on sexual matters to a client?

> Are the arrangements arrived at after consultation with staff, clients and their families?

> Are they explained to all staff, clients and clients' families?

As an aid to the deliberations of care staff, it might be helpful if we reviewed a policy document evolved in one of the hospitals in which we work, following numerous discussions with staff at all levels, and which was finally approved by the administratively responsible committee. This was called 'The Operational Policy on Interpersonal Relationships'. It was one of 30 Operational Policies written out for a new hospital opened in 1971. It has been restated and updated several times since its original appearance. The hospital was planned and built with married quarters of a rather spartan type. The wards were planned and opened as bisexual units, each sex sleeping either side of communal day rooms and dining rooms. It was expected to pass mentally handicapped married couples through into a local guardianship scheme with long-term, supervised boarding-houses and families in the locality, evolved in co-operation with the local social services department.

The first two pages of this Operational Policy described the human need for friendship, social interaction, and sexual interest, which is a normal feature of the human as a gregarious animal. It described how handicapped humans like all others responded to advice and the example set by those around them. It pointed out that care staff, in this case nurses, would be asked questions which they would be expected to answer on the subject of sex and friendships, and suggested that there were four stages at which counselling and consultation might be needed:

1 Friendship   Friendship between humans is to be encouraged, since it stimulates each concerned, aids in their mental development and enthusiasms, and promotes a healthy interest in life and its rich possibilities. Just as normal parents promote friendships with some of their children's adolescent friends and not others, for personal reasons associated with their own hopes and fears for their loved ones, so care staff would be expected to give frank and open reasons why they are doing so, because in this way their charges are most likely to respond.

2 Going steady   Counselling at this stage was suggested as being directed to the emotional side of a friendship which was now making exclusive personal demands on the two concerned. Some parents find it necessary to counsel a weeping adolescent whose boy friend fails to ring her up at the time agreed. In the same way care staff can use this as an aid to teach people to use the telephone, write letters, or ensure time-keeping is learnt well. Both may be taxed by questions: 'What do I do if he kisses me?' 'He wants me to stay out with him!' 'Do you think he loves me?' This is a necessary part of the learning process of life. The couple would need to be counselled that this stage means each is expected to care for the other, pay attention to the other's needs, and not go chasing after any Tom, Dick, Sally or Sue who more interestingly comes on the horizon!

3 Engagement   If a couple request this serious step, a case conference is called in the above hospital for all those concerned in the situation, including, of course, next of kin. Such a meeting emphasizes the seriousness of the step, and discusses what timing is appropriate. The purchase of a ring is apposite, although the couple may need to wait until they have saved the money for this. An arbitrary length of six months is set for an engagement, during which time the staff would now take the initiative in counselling the pair together on what sex means in and out of marriage, the birth-control methods usually needed, exactly what loving will mean to each of the pair concerned, meeting each other's emotional needs, and the art of living together. Domestic training, cooking and budgeting have to be covered and a special time and place may need to be set aside for this. Staff must take the initiative in helping with future plans, including many of the things which married staff realize an unmarried couple might not have discussed. Clearly, even for those on Social Security, the financial aspects are important and the habit of saving may need to be inculcated.

4 Marriage   If all has gone well during the six months, and both are capable and wish to proceed to a wedding, then this is the final stage of counselling in the policy document. There are many problems to be sorted out in the first few months of marriage for normal and handicapped people alike, and both need to learn techniques of lovemaking. Here, staff may need to take the initiative in explanation. Commonly the male reaches his climax far ahead of the female and with the handicapped, as with normal people, this may lead to a good deal of frustration unless the nuances of care are described.

Birth control and sterilization are not a part of the operational document referred to above, for since it was concerned with hospital living the medical staff were expected to take the leading part in this. Vasectomy was usually advised, since it is a simple operation for the male and can be done under a local anaesthetic. If the couple were bright and wished for children at a later stage, a intrauterine device was usually advocated and fitted. The couple were also advised that this needed to be replaced every two years.

What of the future? We see no reason why National Health hospitals should not contain married quarters for the severely mentally handicapped and physically handicapped alike, and see every reason why local-authority hostels and homes should provide bedsitting-rooms for couples, too. It is true that care staff in all types of residential accommodation may not at first see the sexual needs of their clients as their responsibility. We have found that if the matter is discussed with care staff in the absence of upset or crisis, they usually understand the need for release of tension and for personal contentment and are prepared to discuss ways of achieving both. We feel that although married quarters in local-authority accommodation is important, this is only one step in community care. For married couples the next step might be sheltered housing or a flatlet or council house of their own. We like the idea of varieties of sheltered housing that some authorities have evolved for the aged, and we would hope that the same idea could be applied to the physically and multiply handicapped.

Sex education for the handicapped has now been generally accepted and is a very important field in its own right. We hope this book will be an aid to counselling and discussion, for parents and care staff alike, for the gain of all concerned.

Appendix 1

a guide to resources

The audio-visual material on health, hygiene and sex education reviewed here has been selected with three aims in mind. First, to provide theoretical background and 'revision' for parents and professionals. Second, to indicate what might profitably be used with a mentally handicapped audience. Third, to suggest further publications of interest to the reader who wishes to pursue the whole subject in more depth.

Regrettably there is a dearth of British material designed specifically for the mentally handicapped, although there is an increasing amount produced for a wide range of normal children and adolescents. American resources are mentioned only when they are easily obtainable in this country.

The mentally handicapped will need to cover nearly all the topics that normal children do. Many, if not most of us, never had a formal course of hygiene or sex education at school. To bring yourself up to date with the curricula now used in classrooms we suggest that you contact your local education office. Several authorities have published reports of their programmes (Birmingham, Cheshire, Gloucestershire and the ILEA are particularly helpful).

GENERAL SOURCES

* Your local health education officer (contact through your area health authority).
* Your local education officer concerned with special schools.
* The local education department's audio-visual library.
* The nurse training school attached to your local general or mental hospital may be helpful in lending models of body parts and a skeleton.
* A source list of publications and teaching aids in the field of sex education is available from the Health Education Council.
* The Educational Foundation for Visual Aids produces a comprehensive list of audio-visual material for use in schools, etc. Part 6 (ii) of the catalogue on *Human Biology, Hygiene and Health, Teacher Education*, is available from the Educational Foundation for Visual Aids.
* A review of audio-visual resources entitled *Health, Hygiene and Sex Education for Mentally Handicapped Children, Adolescents and Adults* by Ann Craft, is available free from the Health Education Council's Resource Centre, 71–75 New Oxford Street, London WC1A 1AH.

MATERIAL FOR PARENTS, TEACHERS, COUNSELLORS

Books

AMERICAN ASSOCIATION FOR HEALTH, PHYSICAL EDUCATION AND RECREATION, AND SEX INFORMATION AND EDUCATION COUNCIL OF THE UNITED STATES (SIECUS), *A Resource Guide in Sex Education for the Mentally Retarded*, 1971.
Available on loan (by post if necessary) from the Library of International Planned Parenthood Federation. Gives a curriculum guide useful for ESN(M) children and adolescents under the headings: awareness of self; physical changes and understanding self; peer relationships; responsibilities to society as men and women. The resource material listed is solely American.

BALDWIN, D., *Human Biology and Health*, Longman, 1978.
Lots of drawings, photos and ideas for the teacher.

BARNES, K.C., *He and She*, Penguin Books, 1962.
This is a book written for adolescents, but is an excellent reminder of the interests, concerns and problems of young people as they grow up.

BASS, M., *Developing Community Acceptance of Sex Education for the Mentally Retarded*, SIECUS, 1972 (122 East 42nd Street, New York, N.Y. 10017).
Available on loan from International Planned Parenthood Federation. Although written for the American scene it is a useful book for teachers in Special Schools in planning preparatory meetings with parents.

BENDER, M., VALLETUTTI, P. and BENDER, R., *Teaching the Moderately and Severely Handicapped Vol. II Communication, Socialization, Safety, Leisure Time Skills*.
University Park Press, 1976.
An excellent manual with lots of teaching suggestions and strategies.

BURKITT, A., *Man and Woman*, Trident Television, 1977.
Available from Trident House, Brook Mews, London, W1Y 2PN.
Uses clear and simple language to get its information across.

CRAFT, A. and CRAFT, M. (eds), *Sex Education and Counselling for Mentally Handicapped People*, Costello Press, 1982.
Many aspects of the subject are examined. The contributions include a detailed curriculum and teaching strategies.

ELKINGTON, P. and WARD, J., *Biology You Need*, Nelson, 1979.
A workbook for normal youngsters giving lots of ideas about health education.

FAMILY PLANNING ASSOCIATION, *Learning to Live with Sex*, 1972.
A booklet for teenagers in the form of an A–Z of sexuality. Useful as quick 'revision'.

FISCHER, H.L., KRAJICEK, M.J. and BORTHICK, W.A., *Sex Education for the Developmentally Disabled: A Guide for Parents, Teachers and Professionals*, University Park

Press, Baltimore, rev. edn, 1974.
This American workbook may be purchased from H.K. Lewis and Co., Ltd, Medical and Scientific Booksellers and Publishers, 136 Gower Street, London, WC1E 6BS, and other booksellers. It is also available on loan from International Planned Parenthood Federation. The book is designed to ascertain an adolescent's knowledge of body functions and sexual behaviour through recognition of line drawings, and provides a means of introducing teaching on these topics. Has sections on client interviews, parental involvement, and teacher/professional workshops.

GORDON, S., *Sexual Rights for the People Who Happen to be Handicapped*, Center on Human Policy, Syracuse University, Syracuse, New York, 1974.
Straightforward 12-page booklet summing up why, what and how sex education should be given to the mentally handicapped. Available on loan from International Planned Parenthood Federation.

HARRIS, A., *Questions about Sex*, Hutchinson, 1968.
Useful short book (64 pages) written in straightforward style to answer the questions most teenagers want to ask about sex.

HEALTH EDUCATION COUNCIL, *Answering a Child's Questions*, 1973.
Free 8-page booklet setting out helpful guidelines for each age group from birth to late teens.

JENNINGS, S., *Remedial Drama*, Pitman, 1973.
Lots of ideas for teachers to utilize and adapt.

KEMPTON, W., *Guidelines for Planning a Training Course on Human Sexuality and the Retarded*, Philadelphia, Planned Parenthood Association of Southeastern Pennsylvania, 1972.
Available on loan from International Planned Parenthood Federation. The title of this excellent American book is self-explanatory. Has sections on the goals of sex education; answers to parents' questions; concerns of care staff in institutions.

KEMPTON, W., *Sex Education for Persons with Disabilities that Hinder Learning*, Duxbury Press, 1975.
Contains chapters on the teacher's role as educator and

counsellor; the content of sex education; techniques.

KEMPTON, W., BASS, M. and GORDON, S., *Love, Sex and Birth Control for the Mentally Retarded: A Guide for Parents*, Planned Parenthood Association, 1972 (1402 Spruce Street, Philadelphia, PA 19102, USA).

This straightforward and informative 40-page book, designed to cover areas of parental concern, is available on loan from the International Planned Parenthood Federation.

KENNER, J., *Goodbye to the Stork*, National Marriage Guidance Council, 1973.

Excellent small book, dealing sensibly with most aspects of sex education.

ISLINGTON SOCIETY FOR THE MENTALLY HANDICAPPED, *Sex and the Mentally Handicapped: A guide for parents of mentally handicapped people.* Available from 404 Camden Road, London N7.

An 8-page booklet in question-and-answer form written to help parents.

LATTO, K., *Give Us the Chance: sport and physical recreation with mentally handicapped people*, Disabled Living Foundation, 1981.

Contains games and exercises for both the able-bodied and handicapped.

LEE, G., *Sex Education and the Mentally Retarded*, NSMHC, 1976.

Helpful 14-page booklet including short sections on parent involvement, programme-planning, objectives, curriculum.

LOWES, L., *Sex and Social Training: A programme for young adults*, NSMHC, 1977.

A 7-page report of a programme run in an Adult Training Centre.

MITCHELL, L.K., DOCTOR, R.M. and BUTLER, D.C., *A Manual for Behavioral Intervention on the Sexual Problems of Retarded Individuals in Residential or Home Settings.* Available from Ms L. Mitchell, c/o D.C. Butler, Dept. of Psychology, California State University, Northridge, CA 91330, USA.

The manual suggests practical ways of ensuring that sexual behaviour is appropriate to time, place and person.

ORTHO PHARMACEUTICAL CORPORATION, *Under-*

standing Conception and Contraception, 1971.

Useful explanatory material with drawings and diagrams of reproductive system, growth of the baby, and contraceptive methods. Could be selectively used for ESN(M) adolescents. Available from Ortho Pharmaceutical Corporation, Saunderton, High Wycombe, Bucks HP14 4HJ.

POMEROY, W.B., *Boys and Sex*, Pelican Books, 1970.

POMEROY, W.B., *Girls and Sex*, Pelican Books, 1971.

Both books are aimed at adolescent audiences and describe clearly the physical and emotional changes which occur at puberty. Each book ends with the questions most frequently asked by teenagers and gives straightforward answers. Mentally handicapped youngsters may not be as articulate as other adolescents, but they get anxious over many of the same points.

RAYNER, C., *Where do I Come From?*, Arlington Books, 1974.

Small and helpful book with one section on how to answer a child's questions about sex, and another on what to tell him or her. Illustrated with simple line drawings.

ROGERS, R., *Sex Education: Rationale and Reaction*, Cambridge University Press, 1974.

Excellent 'reader' with sections on the theory, practice and effects of sex education and psycho-sexual development.

WARREN, B., *Drama Games for Mentally Handicapped People*, NSMHC, 1981.

Very useful small book to give ideas to the teacher.

WHELAN, E. and SPEAKE, B., *Learning to Cope*, Human Horizon Series, Souvenir Press, 1979.

Has practical suggestions for increasing repertoires of independent behaviour.

SCHOOLS COUNCIL PROJECT: *Health Education*, Nelson, 1977.

All About Me (for 5–8 year olds)

1 Finding out about myself
2 How did I begin?
3 What is growing?
4 What helps me grow?
5 Looking after myself
6 Keeping safe
7 Knowing about others

Think Well (for 9–13 year olds)
1 My self
2 One of many
3 From sickness to health?
4 Deadly decisions
5 Time to spare
6 Food for thought
7 Get clean
8 Skills and spills

Excellent sets of Teacher's Guides with lots of teaching ideas to make learning interesting. Could easily be adapted to suit mentally handicapped youngsters and adults.

SHENNAN, V., *Help Your Child to Understand Sex*, NSMHC, 1976.
Straightforward and helpful 7-page pamphlet written especially for parents.

SPECIAL EDUCATION CURRICULUM DEVELOPMENT CENTER, UNIVERSITY OF IOWA, *Social and Sexual Development: A Guide for Teachers of the Handicapped*, 1972.
Available from Campus Stores, I.M.U. 30, University of Iowa, Iowa City, Iowa 52242, U.S.A.
A 237-page manual of topics and teaching approaches.

Tape/Slide Programmes

CRAFT, A. *Sexual Counselling for Mentally Handicapped People, their Parents and Care Staff.*
CRAFT, A. and CRAFT, M. *Health and Sex Education for the Mentally Handicapped.*
REA, N. *Sexual Needs of the Mentally Handicapped.*
All available for hire or purchase from Graves Medical Audiovisual Library, P.O. Box 99, Chelmsford, Essex, CM2 9BJ.

Films (16 mm)

The ABC of Sex Education for Trainable Persons (Colour, 20 mins, American), Hallmark Films, 1975.

Available on hire from NSMHC.

A little stilted in style, but details why and what sex education is needed by ESN(S) persons.

Caring and Sharing (Colour, 36 mins, Canadian), 1974.

Available from Concord Films Ltd.

By looking at the myths concerning sexuality, the mis-information we all pick up, and the harm this can do in our personal relationships, the film is excellent for preparation and discussion purposes.

The How and What of Sex Education for Educable Persons (Colour, 20 mins, American), Hallmark Films, 1975.

Available on hire from NSMHC. (For ESN(M).)

Like Other People (Colour, 37 mins, British), 1972.

Available from Concord Films Ltd, or the Spastics Society. A film about the emotional and sexual needs of young adult spastics in a residential unit. Many of the difficulties they encounter in their efforts to lead as normal a life as possible also apply to a number of the mentally handicapped living in hospitals and hostels. Thought-provoking and useful for discussion.

What Shall we Tell the Children? (Black and white, 39 mins, Thames TV), 1968.

Available from Concord Films Ltd.

Good discussion starter with professional and parent groups. Reminds us of the haphazard and sometimes damaging way normal children learn the facts of life.

Video cassette

Donal and Sally (Colour, 75 mins, BBC TV), 1979.

Available from Concord Films Ltd.

A very human story of two ATC trainees who wish to pursue their friendship and the reactions of staff and parents.

MATERIAL FOR MENTALLY HANDICAPPED CHILDREN, ADOLESCENTS AND ADULTS

This section is arranged by topic for the reader's convenience.

Conception, pregnancy and birth

Books

'ALTHEA', *A Baby in the Family*, Dinosaur Publications, 1975.
> Conception and childbirth in the context of family love. Explicit and well-drawn illustrations on each page. Introduces and explains correct terminology. Could be used with all age groups.

ANDRY, A.C. and SCHEPP, S., *How Babies Are Made*, Time-Life International, 1969.
> Imaginatively illustrated with a simple text, suitable for younger children. (Perhaps skipping some of the animals!)

CHOVIL, C. and JONES, E.G., *How Did I Grow?*, BBC Publications, 1977.
> Nicely illustrated account of where babies come from, how they are cared for in the womb, etc., based on the BBC Merry-Go-Round Series.

FAGERSTROM, G. and HANSSON, G., *Our New Baby*, Macdonald Educational, 1979.
> A picture story book with mother and father explaining all about the new baby to their little girl and boy. Very realistic with excellent illustrations.

HEMMING, J. and MAXWELL, Z. (eds), *Growing Up*, Macmillan, 1975.
> Has a section on conception and birth with lots of good photographs.

KNUDSEN, P.H., *How a Baby is Made*, Piccolo Picture Books Ltd, 1975.
> Nicely illustrated, shows a loving couple, sexual intercourse, growth of a baby in the womb, birth, breast feeding.

MAYLE, P., *Where Did I Come From?*, Macmillan, 1978.
> Simple text and humorous illustrations. Looks at differences between men and women, making love, pregnancy.

NILSSON, L., *How you Began*, Kestrel Books, 1975.
Lots of splendid photographs with a simple text.
SCHAPP, M. and C., and SHEPARD, S., *Let's Find out About Babies*, Franklin Watts, 1977.
Short simple illustrated text, explaining everyone was once a baby, all babies come from eggs, ovum and sperm, the womb, dependency of the human baby.
SHEFFIELD, M., *Where Do Babies Come From?*, Jonathan Cape, 1973.
Simple and well illustrated text derived from the BBC programme of the same name. Introduces terms such as womb, vagina, penis, sperm.
SPIERS, H., *How you Began*, J.M. Dent, 1971.
Explains how a baby is conceived, born and fed.

Films, slides, video, etc.

How Babies are Born (16 mm colour, 10 mins, British), Eothen Films International Ltd.
An animated film for primary school children introducing both animal and human reproduction and the role of both parents.
Merry Go Round (colour, 20 mins each, BBC), available from BBC Enterprises *or* Video Record off air.
    (i) Beginning
    (ii) Birth
    (iii) Full Circle
The focus is on development, birth, growth of the young human baby. No discussion of marriage, morality or behaviour.
Birth (24 frame slides or filmstrip, cassette and notes), available from Camera Talks Ltd.
Not all the pictures would be understandable, but the last sequence is of an actual birth.
Human Reproduction (43 American colour slides, part of Winifred Kempton's presentations on *Sexuality and the Mentally Handicapped*), available for hire from the FPA or SPOD *or* purchase from Concord Film Council Ltd, or Edward Patterson Assoc. Ltd.
An excellent teacher's aid.

Talking Points, set 2 *Life* (25 10" × 8" b/w photocards), PTM Ltd.

The theme of these stimulus cards is love and affection, intercourse, pregnancy, birth, and care of babies.

Contraception

Books

BALDWIN, D., *Then and Now*, Longman Child Development Series, 1978.

Written for normal youngsters, but could be used with ESN(M) school leavers and adults.

BROOK ADVISORY CENTRES UNIT, *A Look at Safe Sex*, undated.

A 28-page booklet especially designed for the less able and for poor readers.

Illustrates and explains contraceptive methods in simple and explicit language.

Films, slides, video, etc.

The Least You Can Do (16 mm colour, 20 mins, British) part of Granada TV's *Facts for Life* schools programme. Available as film from Concord Films Council Ltd *or* video from Granada Television Ltd.

A very useful review of the methods available.

Contraception (33 slides/filmstrip, cassette and notes) available from Camera Talks Ltd.

A useful introduction, but needs to be supplemented with other material.

Contraceptive Display Kit, Family Planning Association. Samples of contraceptives, useful to use in conjunction with explanatory book or film.

Good health

Books

'ALTHEA', *Going to the Doctor*, Dinosaur Publications, 1973.

Shows a child having a physical examination, getting some medicine, having an X-ray and an injection.

'ALTHEA', *Going into Hospital*, Dinosaur Publications, 1974.

What to expect in the children's ward of a general hospital.

'ALTHEA', *Visiting the Dentist*, Dinosaur Publications, 1974.

How the dentist 'mends' teeth. Shows the different instruments he uses.

The above three books are in an excellent 'What to expect' series for children aged 2-7, but could be used for a wide range of mentally handicapped. All beautifully illustrated.

JOHNSON, V. and WILLIAMS, T., *Good Health*, Book 1, Nelson, 1979.

Based on the ATV 'Good Health' series. Sections on well-being, looking after myself, teeth, leisure activities.

SCHOOLS COUNCIL PROJECT, *What Helps me Grow* and *Looking After Myself*, Units 4 and 5 in the 'All About Me' series. *From Sickness to Health, Deadly Decisions, Time to Spare, Food for Thought*, and *Skills and Spills*, Units 3, 4, 5, 6 and 8 of the 'Think Well' series, Nelson 1977.

Lots of ideas on health education material.

SMITH, T. and BRECKON, B., *Accident Action*, Macmillan, 1978.

Very useful to remind people of causes of accidents, prevention and response.

Films, slides, video, etc.

Let's Go – and Keep Fit and *Let's Go – and Cross the Road* (colour 20 mins video or film). Video available from the BBC or Record Off Air; film available from Concord Films Ltd.

Where There's Smoke (colour 16 mm 14 mins Canadian film) available from Concord Films Ltd.

Cartoon situations making the point that smoking is stupid and harmful.

Accidents Don't Just Happen – They are Caused (30 slides/filmstrip, cassette and notes) available from Camera Talks Ltd.

Before and after sequences involve the audience in recognising the causes of accidents.

Educating Mentally Handicapped People,

2. *The Picture of Health* (51 slides/filmstrip, cassette and notes) available from Camera Talks Ltd.

Stresses the importance of exercise, the proper food, sleep and hygiene.

Good Health for You (37 slides/filmstrip, cassette and notes) available from Camera Talks Ltd.

Useful for discussing personal hygiene, eating the right foods, need for rest, exercise and fresh air.

The Healthy Way in Wonderland

Miss Huff 'n Puff's Exercise Troupe

Chef Ahmalette's Health Diet

(American filmstrips with cassettes) available from The Slide Centre.

The American commentary may need some explanation, but the cartoon characters explain the need for physical fitness, exercise and sleep and secondly a balanced diet with sufficient liquid intake.

Good Health (15 mins video or 16 mm films of the ATV series of the same name) available from ATV Network Ltd *or* Rank Film Library.

2 White Ivory

3 Dr Sweet-Tooth (film title: The Good Food Programme)

4 Love your Lungs

5 Germs, Germs, Germs

6 Watch Out!

7 Fit and Healthy (film title: Exercise and Rest)

8 Talking Feet

9 Time to Spare? (film title: Fun and Games)

All useful to start discussion on health topics.

Growing up

Books

HEALTH EDUCATION COUNCIL, *How We Grow Up*, undated. Free booklet.

An illustrated simple explanation of human development and reproduction.

HEMMING, J. and MAXWELL, Z. (eds), *Achieving Sexual Maturity* and *Growing Up*, Macmillan, 1975.
Well-produced books with plenty of photographs and pictures.

MAYLE, P., *What's Happening to Me?* Macmillan, 1978.
The text is simple and straightforward, and the illustrations are deliberately aimed at humour. Fun to use, but in conjunction with other material.

SCHOOLS COUNCIL PROJECT, *Myself* and *One of Many*, units 1 and 2 in the 'Think Well' series, Nelson, 1977.
These units focus on puberty and sexual development.

Films, slides, video, etc.

What Next? (colour, 15 mins, programme 10 in ATV's 'Good Health' series) available as a video from ATV Network Ltd, *or* 16 mm film from Rank Film Library. Looks at the growth of children during puberty, emphasizing social and emotional relationships.

Growing Up (15 slides, cassette and notes) BBC Radiovision. No longer available from the BBC, but Education Resource Centres may have a copy.
Explains the changes as boys and girls grow up. Uses and explains words such as periods, sanitary towels, penis, testicles, sperm.

Having a Period (42 slides/filmstrip, cassette and notes) No. 3 in the series 'Educating Mentally Handicapped People' available from Camera Talks Ltd.
The emphasis is on the practical management of a period, with a brief biological explanation.

Male Puberty (22 American slides) and *Female Puberty* (45 American slides) Parts II and III of Winifred Kempton's 'Sexuality and the Mentally Handicapped' teaching presentations. Available on loan from the FPA or SPOD, *or* purchase from Concord Film Council Ltd or E. Patterson Assoc. Ltd.
The slides illustrate body changes, hygiene, erections, menstruation, masturbation.

Feminine Hygiene Educational Kit (37 frame filmstrip, cassette, teacher's notes, leaflets, calendar, samples of sanitary pads, etc.) available from Robinson's, Wheatbridge Mills, Chesterfield, Derbyshire.

A very useful teaching aid designed as an introduction to menstruation for normal 8- to 12-year-old girls.

The human body

Books

CLARK, P.M. and BURGESS, J. (eds) *You and Your Body*, Macmillan, 1979.

Lots of illustrations and a simple text covering the family, the body, illness and growing up.

DANIEL, D.S., *Your Body*, Ladybird Books, 1967 (also available as a 25 frame colour filmstrip).

Contains coloured pictures of a skeleton, skin, digestion, the five sense etc.

HALFORD, S., *Teeth*, Ladybird Books, 1978 (also available as a colour filmstrip).

Lots of nice illustrations and simple texts showing animal and human teeth, and a story of tooth decay.

MOYLE, D. (ed) *The Human Body*, Macdonald Educational, Easy Reading Edition, 1975.

Colourfully illustrated book with large print. Has sections on bones, muscles, skin, etc.

RAYNER, C. *The Body Book*, G. Wizzard/Andre Deutsch, 1978.

Written for very young children, but could be used with ESN people. Teachers might be wise to substitute some of the terms, e.g. 'vagina' for 'baby making hole'.

THOMAS, G.D.B., *How your Body Works*, Hulton Educational Publications, 1964.

A Read and Discover Book with simple text and suggestions for the reader, e.g. taking a pulse, tasting food blindfolded.

Films, slides, video, etc.

Growing Up Day by Day (colour, 14 mins, 16 mm American film) available from Fergus Davidson Associates Ltd.

Looks at children at an 8-year-old boy's birthday party. Everyone grows at different rates.

Discovering your Senses (6 American filmstrips, cassettes and notes)
    Your Eyes are for Seeing
    Your Ears are for Hearing
    Your Skin is for Feeling
    Your Tongue is for Tasting
    Your Nose is for Smelling
    Your Senses Work Together
    Available from Gateway Educational Media.
    The American commentary may need explanation, but the series is excellent. The notes suggest post-showing activities.

The Five Senses (4 × 12 slides with teacher's notes) available from The Slide Centre Ltd.
    Hearing
    Sight
    Touch
    Smell and Taste
    Illustrates the work of the senses.

Inside the Body (32 frame colour filmstrip, cassette and notes) BBC 'Life Cycle' Radiovision. Available from BBC Publications.
    Uses X-ray pictures and photographs to show structure and function of the skeleton and various organs.

You and Your Health (American filmstrips, cassettes and notes) available from The Slide Centre Ltd.
    You – and Your Sense of Smell and Taste.
    You – and Your Sense of Touch
    You – the Living Machine
    The American commentary may need explanation, but the cartoon format is fun to use.

Who Am I? 34 slides/filmstrip, cassette and notes. No. 7 in the 'Live and Learn' series) available from Camera Talks Ltd.
    Uses children's drawings to illustrate aspects of human biology.

Parts of the Body (35 American slides) Part I of Winifred Kempton's teaching presentation on 'Sexuality and the Mentally Handicapped'. Available on loan from the FPA or SPOD, *or* purchase from Concord Film Council Ltd. or E. Patterson Assoc. Ltd.
    Particularly helpful for sexual body parts.

Body Parts Dice Game (playing board 30 × 40 cm) available from Taskmaster.
Designed to teach and reinforce the names of 21 important body parts.

Digesting our Food (large chart, 76 × 100 cm) available from Pictorial Charts Educational Trust.
Outline of a man showing the digestive system and how long it takes for a meal to pass through the body.

Human Skeleton (white outline on linen backed blackboard paper, 40 × 30 ins) available from T. Gerrard and Co.

BE BA BO Image Unit (folding flannel board, 33 × 48 ins, child-size flannel body parts, teacher's manual and 20 activity units) available from Living and Learning.
Useful for teaching ESN(S) people to identify various parts of the body.

Large Body Puzzles (printed in colour on heavy board stock. Each clothed figure measures approximately 4 ft. Black girl puzzle has 25 pieces, white boy has 31) available from Taskmaster.
Useful exercise for ESN(S) pupils.

Human Body Parts Flannel Aid (five 16-inch figures with 32 coloured flannel pieces of body parts and clothing, together with 23 name cards). Available from Living and Learning.
Useful for helping pupils to name and recognize parts of the body.

Human Body (12-inch model with clear plastic 'skin'. Comes apart and all main organs are removable.) Available from Living and Learning.
Fairly dexterous hands and fingers needed, but fun to show.

Human Skeleton (12-inch model on a stand) available from Living and Learning.
Even a small three-dimensional model can be useful to supplement pictures.

Topsy Giant Jigsaw (large wooden pieces, comprising girl's head, boy's head, trunk, two arms, two legs, to peg on board, 22" × 32") available from ESA Creative Learning Ltd.
Helpful as a resource in a Special School to aid body recognition.

Personal hygiene

Books

HOLT, A. and RANDELL, J., *Come Clean*, Cambridge University Press, 1975.
24-page book with illustrations and simple text on aspects of hygiene.

SCHOOLS COUNCIL PROJECT, *Get Clean*, Unit 7 of the 'Think Well' series, Nelson, 1977.
Aspects of hygiene, and care of teeth and feet.

HEALTH EDUCATION COUNCIL, *Are you a Stinker?* (free leaflet).
Looks at personal freshness and highlights the parts of the body which need special attention.

Films, slides, video, etc.

Keeping Neat and Clean (colour, 11 mins, 16 mm American film) available from Fergus Davidson Associates Ltd.
Shows the importance of bathing and putting on clean clothes.

Let's Go – and Get Ready and *Let's Go – and Look After our Teeth* (20 mins video or film of BBC programme).
Record Off Air *or* Concord Films Ltd.

About your Feet (31 frame filmstrip and notes. Family Doctor filmstrip). Available from Educational Audio-visual Ltd.
How feet should be looked after.

Educating Mentally Handicapped People (slides/filmstrips, cassettes and notes) available from Camera Talks Ltd.
2. The Picture of Health
3. Having a Period
Both illustrate the need to wash or bath carefully and regularly.

The Healthy Way in Wonderland (American filmstrips, cassettes and notes) available from The Slide Centre.
Rub a Dub Dub
The Neat Bird
The Wizard of Good Appearance
The American commentaries may need explanation, the cartoon characters make learning fun.

Self-Care Sequential Cards (four sequences of six coloured cards, 76 × 102 mm) available from Taskmaster.
All focus on grooming and hygiene.

Personal relationships

Books

ANGLUND, J.W., *Love is a Special Way of Feeling*, Collins, 1960.
A beautifully produced little book with charming illustrations. It attempts to describe the various aspects of love and how we feel.

HOLT, A. and RANDELL, J., *The Two of Us*, Cambridge University Press, 1976.
A work book on relationships, especially designed for the less-able pupil, so lots of ideas to use for the mentally handicapped group.

MAYLE, P., *Will I Like It?*, W.H. Allen, 1978.
A helpful book to use in counselling with those known to be sexually active.

ROBERTS, R., *Families*, Nelson, 1978.
One of eight booklets accompanying the ATV series 'Alive and Kicking'. Nicely illustrated with a simple text looking at human and animal families.

SCHOOLS COUNCIL PROJECT, *Knowing About Others*, Unit 7 in the 'All About Me' series, Nelson, 1977, and *One of Many*, Unit 2 in the 'Think Well' series, Nelson, 1977.
Both look at relationships within the family and outside, and growing responsibilities.

Films, slides, video, etc.

Are We Still Going to the Movies? (colour, 14 mins 16 mm American film) available from McGraw Hill Books (UK) Ltd or Concord Films Ltd.
Teenage girl and boy on a picnic. He wants to make love, she doesn't. What is love? Is sex the whole point of a relationship?

Good Health (15 mins video available from ATV Network Ltd or 16 mm film available from Rank Film Library).

1. Everybody's Different (explores the differences and similarities between people and individual responsibility).
10. What Next? (the growth of children during puberty, emphasizing social and emotional relationships).
12. Summer Camp (looks at three boys and their feelings of jealousy, hostility, responsibility and friendship).

Behave Yourself! (50 slides/filmstrip, cassette and notes. No. 1 in the 'Educating Mentally Handicapped People' series) available from Camera Talks Ltd.
Looks at good manners and good behaviour, ends by posing some moral dilemmas to promote audience discussion.

Good Manners are Me (American filmstrips, cassettes and notes) available from Gateway Educational Media.
Me, Myself and I.
I Live with People
I Have Friends
Made for primary schoolchildren, covering personal hygiene, neatness, manners, posture and courtesy. Lots of discussion points.

Me and My Family (American filmstrips, cassettes and notes) available from Gateway Educational Media.
It's Not Fair!
Why Can't I?
Please Listen!
Angry Words, Angry Feelings
It's Your Fault!
That's Mine!
All focus on areas of stress in family relationships. The American dialogue may need explanation, but the emphasis is on give and take and problem solving without recourse to angry words.

Social Behaviour (40 American slides). Part IV of Winifred Kempton's teaching presentation on 'Sexuality and the Mentally Handicapped'. Available on loan from FPA or SPOD, *or* purchase from Concord Films Ltd or E. Patterson Assoc. Ltd.
Looks at dating, appropriate behaviour, homosexuality.

Values: Right or Wrong (six American filmstrips, cassettes and teacher's notes) available from Fergus Davidson Associated Ltd.

107

Why Rules?
What is Responsibility?
What is Honesty?
Why Play Fair?
What is Yours, What is Mine?
What is Appreciating Others?
Made for children of Junior School age, useful for an older group to provoke decisions about the stories and discussion.

See How you Feel (20 discussion and 30 domino cards) available from Learning Development Aids.
Pictures of non-verbal cues of facial expression and body posture that signal different emotions. Can be played as a game.

This is Me (32 coloured cards, 28 X 23 cm with a picture on each side) available from Taskmaster.
Nearly all the pictures are suitable for mentally handicapped children and adolescents to prompt discussion on feelings and reactions of themselves and others.

GENERAL PUBLICATIONS

For those interested in reading further on the general subject of sexuality and the mentally handicapped the following publications are of interest.

Books

BASS, M. and GELOF, M. (eds), *Sexual Rights and Responsibilities of the Mentally Retarded*, Proceedings of the Conference of the American Association on Mental Deficiency, Region IX. 1972; revd edn, 1975. Available on loan from the International Planned Parenthood Federation.

CRAFT, A. and CRAFT, M. *Handicapped Married Couples*, Routledge & Kegan Paul, 1979.

DAY, K. *The Special Child – The Teenage Years*, Trident Television Ltd, 1979, P.O. Box, Newcastle-upon-Tyne, NE99 1TN.

DE LA CRUZ, F.F. and LA VECK, G.D. (eds), *Human Sexuality and the Mentally Retarded*, Butterworth, 1973.

GREENGROSS, W., *Entitled to Love*, Malaby Press, 1976, ch. 9 (Special Problems of the Mentally Handicapped).

LEE, G.W. and KATZ, G., *Sexual Rights of the Retarded*, NSMHC, 1974.

MATTINSON, J., *Marriage and Mental Handicap*, Institute of Marital Studies, The Tavistock Institute of Human Relations, 1975 (2nd edition).

Articles

BROWN, H., 'Sexual Knowledge and Education of ESN Students in Centers of Further Education', *Sexuality and Disability*, vol. 3, no. 3, pp. 215-20, 1980.

CRAFT, A. and CRAFT, M., 'Subnormality in Marriage: Happiness and the Quality of Life Among Married Subnormals', *Social Work Today*, vol. 7, no. 4, pp. 98-101, 1976.

CRAFT, A. and CRAFT, M., 'Partnership and Marriage for the Subnormal?', *Apex*, vol. 3, no. 2, 1975.

CRAFT, A. and CRAFT, M., 'Personal Relationships and Partnerships for the Mentally Handicapped', ch. in CRAFT, M. (ed.), *Tredgold's Mental Retardation*, 12th edition, Baillière Tindall, 1979.

DAVID, H.P., SMITH, J.D. and FRIEDMAN, E., 'Family Planning Services for Persons Handicapped by Mental Retardation', *American Journal of Public Health*, vol. 66, no. 11, pp. 1053-7, 1976.

EDMONSON, B., McCOMBS, K. and WISH, J., 'What Retarded Adults Believe about Sex', *American Journal of Mental Deficiency*, vol. 84, no. 1, pp. 11-18, 1979.

FISCHER, H.L. and KRAJICEK, M.J., 'Sexual Development of the Moderately Retarded Child: Level of Information and Parental Attitudes', *Mental Retardation*, vol. 12 no. 3, pp. 28-30, 1974.

HALL, J.E., 'Sexual Behaviour', in J. Wortis (ed.), *Mental Retardation (and Developmental Disabilities). An Annual Review*, vol. VI, Brunner/Mazel, 1974.

HALL, J.E., 'Acceptance of Sexual Expression in the Mentally Retarded', *Sexuality and Disability*, vol. 1, no. 1, pp. 44-51, 1978.

HALL, J.E. and MORRIS, H.L., 'Sexual Knowledge and Attitudes of Institutionalized and Noninstitutionalized Retarded Adolescents', *American Journal of Mental Deficiency*, vol. 80, no. 4, pp. 382–7, 1976.

HAMMAR, S.L., WRIGHT, L.S. and JENSEN, D.L., 'Sex Education for the Retarded Adolescent: A Survey of Parental Attitudes and Methods of Management in 50 Retarded Adolescents', *Clinical Pediatrics*, vol. 6, pp. 621–7, 1967.

HARTMAN, S.S. and HYNES, J., 'Marriage Education for Mentally Retarded Adults', Social Casework, pp. 280–4, May, 1975.

JOHNSON, W.R., 'Sex Education and the Mentally Retarded', *Journal of Sex Research*, vol. 5, no. 3, pp. 179–85, 1969.

JONES, A.W., 'Sex and the Mentally Handicapped', *Teaching and Training*, Autumn 1973, pp. 128–35.

KEMPTON, W., 'Sex Education for the Mentally Retarded', *Sexuality and Disability*, vol. 1, no. 2, pp. 137–44, 1978.

MacLEAN, R., 'Sexual Problems and Family Planning Needs of the Mentally Handicapped in Residential Care', *British Journal of Family Planning*, vol. 4, no. 4, pp. 13–15, 1979.

MEYEN, E.L. and RETISH, P.M., 'Sex Education for the Mentally Retarded: Influencing Teachers' Attitudes', *Mental Retardation*, vol. 9, no. 1, pp. 46–9, 1971.

MITCHELL, L., DOCTOR, R.M. and BUTLER, D.C., 'Attitudes of Caretakers toward the Sexual Behavior of Mentally Retarded Persons' *American Journal of Mental Deficiency*, vol. 83, no. 3, pp. 289–96, 1978.

MORGAN, M., 'Attitudes Towards the Sexuality of Handicapped Boys and Girls', paper presented at the Guild of Teachers of Backward Children National Conference, 1972.

MULHERN, T.J., 'Survey of Reported Sexual Behaviour and Policies Characterising Residential Facilities for Retarded Citizens', *American Journal of Mental Deficiency*, vol. 79, no. 6, pp. 670–3, 1975.

PERSKE, R., 'The Dignity of Risk and the Mentally Retarded', *Mental Retardation*, vol. 10, no. 1, pp. 25–7, 1972.

ROSEN, M., 'Conditioning Appropriate Heterosexual Behaviour in Mentally and Socially Handicapped Populations',

Training School Bulletin, vol. 66, pp. 172-7, 1970.
SANDTNER, E.S., 'Sexual Expectations of the Mentally Retarded', *Mental Retardation*, January 1972, pp. 27-9.
SAUNDERS, E.J., 'Staff Members' Attitudes toward the Sexual Behavior of Mentally Retarded Residents', *American Journal of Mental Deficiency*, vol. 84, no. 2, pp. 206-8, 1979.
SHEARER, A., 'A Right to Love?', report on public and professional attitudes towards the sexual and emotional needs of handicapped people, published jointly by the Spastics Society and NAMH, 1972.
WILSON, R.R. and BALDWIN, B.A., 'A Pilot Sexuality Training Workshop for Staff at an Institution for the Mentally Retarded', *American Journal of Public Health*, vol. 66, no. 1, pp. 77-8, 1976.

Addresses

ATV Network Limited
Rutland House
Edmund Street
BIRMINGHAM 3

BBC Enterprises
Villiers House
Broadway
Ealing
LONDON

BBC Publications
School Order Section
144-152 Bermondsey Street
LONDON
SE1 3TH

Brook Advisory Centres Unit
10 Albert Street
BIRMINGHAM
B4 7UD

Camera Talks Limited
31 North Row
LONDON
W1R 2EM

Concord Films Council Limited
201 Felixstowe Road
IPSWICH
IP3 9BJ

Educational Audio Visual Limited
Butterley Street
LEEDS
LS10 1AX

Eothen Films Limited
EMI Film Studios
Shenley Road
BOREHAM WOOD
Herts
WD6 1JG

ESA Creative Learning Ltd.
Pinnacles,
P.O. Box 22
HARLOW
Essex
CM19 5AY

Family Planning Association
27-35 Mortimer Street,
LONDON
W1

Fergus Davidson Associates Limited
1 Bensham Lane
CROYDON
CRO 2RU

Gateway Educational Media
Waverley Road
Yate
BRISTOL
BS17 5RB

T. Gerrard & Co.
Gerrard House
Worthing Road
EAST PRESTON
Nr Littlehampton
Sussex

Learning Development Aids (LDA)
Aware House
Duke Street
WISBECH
Cambs
PE13 2AE

Living and Learning
Church Walk
Kingscliffe
PETERBOROUGH
PE8 6XD

McGraw Hill Books (UK) Limited
Shoppenhangers Road
MAIDENHEAD
Berks
SL6 2QL

NSMHC (now Royal Society for Mentally Handicapped
Children and Adults)
123 Golden Lane
LONDON EC1Y ORT

Edward Patterson Associates Limited
68 Copers Cope Road
BECKENHAM
Kent

Photographic Teaching Materials (PTM)
23 Horn Street
Winslow
BUCKINGHAM
MK18 3AP

Pictorial Charts Educational Trust
27 Kirchen Road
LONDON
W13 OUD

Rank Film Library
PO Box 70
Great West Road
BRENTFORD
Middlesex TW8 9HR

The Slide Centre
143 Chatham Road
LONDON
SW11 6SR

SPOD
The Diorama
14 Peto Place
LONDON
NW1 4DT

Taskmaster
Morris Road
Clarendon Park
LEICESTER
LE2 6BR

Appendix 2

courses and workshops

Although the sexuality of the mentally handicapped has been a much neglected area, there are many signs that professional and parent groups are increasingly anxious to explore the implications of the new climate. For example, the Family Planning Association, in co-operation with MIND and the National Society for Mentally Handicapped Children run 3-day and 5-day courses to teachers and carers of ESN (M) young people. These can be organized on request anywhere in Britain and are based on seminars, group discussions and specialist lectures. Full details are available from the education unit, Family Planning Association.

In the USA Winifred Kempton and Rose Forman have had much experience in planning courses and workshops on human sexuality and mental retardation for parents and professionals. Their suggestion and guidelines are of great value to those who wish to hold similar events.[1] They suggest that each education training course needs to include:

1. Factual information, especially to correct myths and mis-information.
2. Exploration of attitudes, and help with improving the comfort level of the trainees with the subject matter.

3. Suggested techniques and the resources available.
4. Consideration of the special needs and characteristics of the target group.

Each session should have three parts. The first part should present factual material with some opportunity for questions and exchange of ideas and opinions. The second part should focus on the feelings of the participants and encourage them to examine their own comfort levels and attitudes towards sexuality. The third part should offer the participants communication and teaching techniques, suggest practice exercises to attain skill and list the resources needed to counsel or teach sex education to the mentally handicapped. Ideally the size of the group would be less than 25 participants; larger groups could be sub-divided.

They go on to outline nine sessions which could be expanded or contracted according to the time available. The following is a summary of their outline for the sessions:

Session 1   *Introductory Session*
Help participants establish rapport.
Clarify purpose and goals of course.
Establish realistic expectations of course and plans for its use with participants.
Establish goals and philosophy of sex education for the mentally handicapped; dispel myths and relieve anxieties.

Session 2   *Knowledge About Sexuality – Filling the Gaps*
Male and female anatomies.
Facts on reproduction.
Medical aspects of the sexuality of the mentally handicapped.
Human sexual behaviour and human sexual response.
Genetic counselling.
Venereal disease.
Masturbation.

Session 3   *Personal Examination of Attitudes Toward Sexuality*
Main goals: help participants become more comfortable about human sexuality; and develop

116

their skill in communicating about it.
Session should include:

a. Several 'shocking' experiences: the first, involving use of 'sexual language'; the second, instigating self-awareness and areas of discomfort by use of films. Follow films with small group discussions to help alleviate tensions.

b. Discussion of psycho-sexual development to deepen understanding of attitude formation.

Session 4 *Sex Education for the Mentally Handicapped*

a. Questions to be answered: What is sex education? What are its goals? When, how, by whom should it be offered?

b. Special considerations for presenting sex education to those who are ESN(S) and ESN(M). Techniques for presentation.

Session 5 *Helping Parents Deal With the Sexuality of their Mentally Handicapped Child*

Questions and answers specifically concerning the parents of the mentally handicapped. Characteristics and problems that they share with other parents, and differences. How they can best be helped by the professional. Educational and training programmes for parents.

Session 6 *Socialization of the Mentally Handicapped – Dating, Marriage, and Parenthood*

Special issues that confront most mentally handicapped and their parents and advisers in the decisions of whether to marry and whether to have children. The viewpoints of the mentally handicapped themselves, their parents, their children, and the community.

Session 7 *Birth Control for the Mentally Handicapped*

a. Discussion of the various methods of birth control now available that are suitable for the mentally handicapped girl or woman: the Pill, intrauterine device, injection, sterilization and abortion. The medical, psychological, social and legal implications of each method. Use of vasectomy for men.

b. Review of the resources available in the community for birth-control services. Guidelines for effective referrals, counselling, and preparation of client before receiving birth-control services.

Session 8   *Special Considerations Relating to the Sexuality of the Institutionalized Mentally Handicapped*

Examination of the most prevalent problems involving sexual behaviour of the residents: masturbation; homosexuality; and heterosexual contacts. Sex education for the entire staff of the institution in order to encourage more rational attitudes and consistency in dealing with the sexual behaviour of the residents.

Session 9   *Special Topics, such as Legal Rights, Cultural and Religious Implications, Sexual Rights and Responsibilities. Others to be selected by the participants.*

Participants to have the opportunity to explore topics already discussed, in greater detail, if they so desire. Opportunity to introduce subject matter that has not been covered.

Setting Up Sex-Education Programmes

Guidelines to give participants direction in planning for their own settings.

Evaluation and Testing

A summary of the course, its effect on the participants, and more tests to learn what has been accomplished.

Along similar lines is the seven-session workshop programme outlined in a manual produced by the Carolina Population Center.[2] Again, we give a summary:

Topic 1   *Normalization – Changes in Institutions, Opportunities in the Community*

The implications of normalization, ways and means of informing and educating ourselves and the community about the rights and needs of mentally retarded persons in all areas of life including that of sexuality.

Topic 2   *Myths and Facts About Mental Retardation and Sexuality*
Providing participants with up-to-date factual information to help them sort out fact from fiction in an area where myths and misconceptions abound.

Topic 3   *Development of Sexual Attitudes*
Exploration of the origin and development of attitudes about sexuality and how attitudes determine our actions. This session would include a small group exercise to help participants become more aware of their own attitudes and opinions about sex.

Topic 4   *Techniques for Sexuality Counselling, How to Communicate Effectively with the Person Being Counselled*
Role play would be used here.

Topic 5   *Dating, Marriage and Parenthood – Rights and Capabilities of Mentally Retarded Persons*
Showing a film such as *Like Other People*, followed by group discussions.

Topic 6   *Sterilization and the Sexual Rights and Responsibilities of Mentally Retarded Persons*
Discussion of the current legal position. (In Britain involuntary sterilization is illegal but there is the vexed question of 'informed consent'.)

Topic 7   *Teaching Appropriate Sexual Behaviour and Contraceptive Counselling*
Techniques for teaching appropriate behaviour for mentally retarded people of different functioning levels. An examination of the pros and cons of various contraceptive methods for retarded people.

It is essential to plan carefully – human sexuality is a subject where participants are liable to go off at all sorts of tangents unless the day or session is well structured. It is also a subject which can arouse personal anxiety and disquiet. It is probable that some will discover they would not be at ease discussing sexual matters with mentally handicapped people. This is in no way a personal failure, or a course failure, but a sensible and realistic conclusion. Far better to find out right at the outset, without commitments being made, than to communicate nothing but embarrassment later on. In this context it is interesting to note that even in Sweden, where sex education in schools has been compulsory since 1956, a recent report showed that only 20 per cent of teachers expressed interest in that part of the curriculum.

We hope these guidelines will be of use to those considering holding courses and workshops.

Notes

Chapter 1   Myths and morals: the literature

For a comprehensive review of the subject see A. Craft and M. Craft, 'Sexuality and Mental Handicap: A Review', *British Journal of Psychiatry*, vol. 139, pp. 494-505, 1981.

1 B. Kirman and J. Bicknell, *Mental Handicap*, Churchill Livingstone, Edinburgh, 1975.
2 J.E. Hall, 'Sexual Behaviour', in J. Wortis (ed.), *Mental Retardation (and Developmental Disabilities). An Annual Review*, vol. VI, Brunner/Mazel, New York, 1974.
3 E.W. Reed and S.C. Reed, *Mental Retardation: A Family Study*, W.B. Saunders, Philadelphia, 1965.
4 Kirman and Bicknell, *op. cit.*
5 Hall, *op. cit.*
6 P. Mickelson, 'The Feebleminded Parent: A Study of 90 Family Cases', *American Journal of Mental Deficiency*, vol. 51, pp. 644-53, 1947.
7 See A.M. Clarke and A.D.B. Clarke, *Mental Deficiency: The Changing Outlook*, Methuen, London, 2nd edn, 1965; and M.J. Craft, 'Personality Disorder and Dullness', *Lancet*, pp. 856-8, 25 April 1959.
8 R.B. Edgerton and H.F. Dingman, 'Good Reasons for Bad Supervision: "Dating" in a Hospital for the Mentally Retarded', *Psychiatric Quarterly* (supplement), part 2, pp. 1-13, 1964.

Chapter 2 Is ignorance bliss? Sex education, counselling and family-planning services

1 The mentally handicapped are not alone in receiving solely negative advice. An 18 year old boy in Schofield's survey summed up the only sex education he had received at school: 'Before we left the reverend told us not to do it, the doctor told us how not to do it, and the head told us where not to do it.' See M. Schofield, *The Sexual Behaviour of Young People*, Pelican Books, Harmondsworth, 1968.
2 W. Johnson, 'Sex Education and the Mentally Retarded', *Journal of Sex Research*, vol. 5, no. 3, pp. 179–85, 1969.
3 *Op. cit.*
4 A. Harris, 'What Does "Sex Education" Mean?', in R. Rodgers (ed.), *Sex Education: Rationale and Reaction*, Cambridge University Press, 1974.
5 W. Kempton, *Guidelines for Planning a Training Course on Human Sexuality and the Retarded*, Planned Parenthood Association of Southeastern Pennsylvania, Philadelphia, 1972.
6 S. Gordon, 'Symposium on Sex Education', *Journal of Special Education*, vol. 5, no. 4, pp. 351–81, 1972.
7 A. Craft and M.J. Craft, 'Subnormality in Marriage: Happiness and the Quality of Life Among Married Subnormals', *Social Work Today*, vol. 7, no. 4, pp. 98–101, 1976.
8 H.P. David, J.D. Smith and E. Friedman, 'Family Planning Services for Persons Handicapped by Mental Retardation', *American Journal of Public Health*, vol. 66, no. 11, pp. 1053–7, 1976.

Further references

A. Craft, 'Sexual Counselling for Mentally Handicapped People, their Parents and Care Staff', Cassette talk and slides available from Graves Medical Audiovisual Library, P.O. Box 99, Chelmsford, Essex, CM2 9BJ.

A. Craft and M.J. Craft (eds), *Sex Education and Counselling for Mentally Handicapped People*, Costello Press, Tunbridge Wells, 1982.

R. Maclean, 'Birth Control Techniques and Counselling for a Mentally Handicapped Population', in A. Craft and M.J. Craft (eds), *op. cit.*

Chapter 3 Psycho-sexual development

1 H. Williamson, *Donkey Boy*, Panther Books, St Albans, 1962.
2 P. Roth, *Portnoy's Complaint*, Jonathan Cape, London, 1969.

3 J. Bowlby, *Maternal Care and Mental Health*, WHO, Geneva, 1951.
4 For a discussion of this in the context of psycho-sexual problems see T. Main, 'Impotence', in H. Milne and S.J. Hardy (eds), *Psycho-Sexual Problems*, Bradford University Press in association with Crosby Lockwood Staples, London, 1976, ch. 7.
5 P. Righton, 'Sex and the Residential Social Worker', *Social Work Today*, vol. 8, no. 19, p. 12, 1977.
6 L.F. Davis, 'Touch, Sexuality and Power in Residential Settings', *British Journal of Social Work*, vol. 5, no. 4, pp. 397–411, 1975.
7 T.J. Mulhern, 'Survey of Reported Sexual Behaviour and Policies Characterising Residential Facilities for Retarded Citizens', *American Journal of Mental Deficiency*, vol. 79, no. 6, pp. 670–3, 1975.
8 M. Rosen, 'Conditioning Appropriate Heterosexual Behaviour in Mentally and Socially Handicapped Populations', *Training School Bulletin*, vol. 66, pp. 172–7, 1970.
9 J. Vanier, 'Love Is Being Together', *Parents' Voice*, vol. 25, no. 3, 1975.

Chapter 5   Love and the mentally handicapped

1 To preserve anonymity fictitious names have been used throughout the book.
2 They are now happily married and are living in a council maisonette.

Chapter 6   Marriage and the mentally handicapped

This chapter is an expanded version of the authors' 'Subnormality in Marriage: Happiness and the Quality of Life Among Married Subnormals', *Social Work Today*, vol. 7, no. 4, pp. 98–101, 1976; and 'Partnership and Marriage for the Subnormal?' *Apex*, Journal of the Institute of Mental Subnormality, vol. 3, no. 2, 1975.
1 J. Mattinson, *Marriage and Mental Handicap*, Institute of Marital Studies, Tavistock Institute of Human Relations, London, 2nd edn, 1975 (first published 1970).
2 *Op. cit.*
3 For those interested in looking in more detail at the subject of marriage and the mentally handicapped a review of the relevant literature appears in the authors' *Handicapped Married Couples*, Routledge & Kegan Paul, London, 1979.

Chapter 7   The law

This chapter is based on a memorandum entitled 'Law Concerning Sex and the Handicapped', prepared for discussion purposes by M.J. Craft and J.G. Abelson.

1   R. v. Baskerville (1916), 2 KB 658.

Chapter 8   Setting up a health and sex-education programme

1   W. Kempton, *Guidelines for Planning a Training Course on Human Sexuality and the Retarded.* Planned Parenthood Association of Southeastern Pennsylvania, Philadelphia, 1972.

2   H.L. Fischer and M.J. Krajicek, 'Sexual Development of the Moderately Retarded Child: Levels of Information and Parental Attitudes', *Mental Retardation*, vol. 12, no. 3, pp. 28-30, 1974; and J.E. Hall, H.L. Morris and H.R. Barker, 'Sexual Knowledge and Attitudes of Mentally Retarded Adolescents', *American Journal of Mental Deficiency*, vol. 77, no. 6, pp. 706-9, 1973.

3   H.L. Fischer, M.J. Krajicek and W.A. Borthick, *Sex Education for the Developmentally Disabled: A Guide for Parents, Teachers and Professionals*, University Park Press, Boston and London, revised edn, 1974.

4   A.W. Pattullo and K.E. Barnard, 'Teaching Menstrual Hygiene to the Mentally Retarded', *American Journal of Nursing*, Vol. 68, no. 12, 2572-5, 1968.

5   W. Kempton, *Sex Education for Persons with Disabilities that Hinder Learning*, Planned Parenthood Association of Southeastern Pennsylvania, Philadelphia, 2nd edn, 1980.

6   B. Warren, *Drama Games for Mentally Handicapped People*, RSMHC A, London, 1981.

7   S. Hamre-Nietupski and W. Williams, 'Implementation of Selected Sex Education and Social Skills to Severely Handicapped Students', *Education and Training of the Mentally Retarded*, Vol. 12, pp. 364-72, 1977.

8   L.K. Mitchell, R.M. Doctor and D.C. Butler, *A Manual for Behavioral Intervention on the Sexual Problems of Retarded Individuals in Residential or Home Settings.* Purchase from Ms L. Mitchell, c/o D.C. Butler, Department of Psychology, California State University, Northridge, CA 91330, USA.

9   A. Craft, J. Davis, M. Williams and M. Williams, 'A Health and Sex Education Programme: Curriculum and Resources', Chapter in A. Craft and M. Craft (eds), *Sex Education and Counselling for Mentally Handicapped People*, Costello Press, Tunbridge Wells, 1982.

Conclusion

National Development Group for the Mentally Handicapped. *Improving the Quality of Services for Mentally Handicapped People: a Checklist of Standards*, DHSS, London, 1980.

Appendix 2:   Courses and workshops

1 W. Kempton and R. Forman, *Guidelines for Training in Sexuality and the Mentally Handicapped*, Planned Parenthood Association of Southeastern Pennsylvania, 2nd edn, 1976 (1220 Sansom Street, Philadelphia, Pennsylvania 19107, USA).
2 K. Rolett, *Organizing Community Resources in Sexuality Counselling and Family Planning for the Retarded: A Community Workers' Manual*, Carolina Population Center, 1976 (University Square 300-A, Chapel Hill, N. Carolina 27514, USA).

Index

DATE DUE

NOV 1 1 1983	OCT 2 9 1997	
NOV 1 0 1984	NOV 1 7 1997	
APR 1 6 1985	NOV 1 6 2006	
DEC 1 4 1985	NUV 4 0 ZUIZ	
NOV 1 9 1986	MAR 0 3 2014	
DEC 0 1 1986	MAR 2 4 2014	
JAN 9 1986	MAR 2 9 2015	
JAN 0 9 1991		
NOV 0 9 1992		
DEC 1 3 1992		
JAN 0 6 1993		
MAR 1 3 1995		
OCT 1 1 1995		
OCT 2 4 1995		
NOV 1 3 1995		
DEC 1 1995		
NOV 2 4 1996		

HIGHSMITH 45-102   PRINTED IN U.S.A.